GUIDE TO DISPUTE SETTLEM

Diana Páez Wajardo

www.worldtradelaw.net

WTO GUIDE SERIES

Guide to Dispute Settlement

Peter Gallagher

London • The Hague • Boston

Published by Kluwer Law International
P.O. Box 85889, 2508 CN The Hague, The Netherlands.

Sold and distributed in the U.S.A. and Canada
by Kluwer Law International,
101 Philip Drive, Norwell, MA 02061, U.S.A.

In all other countries, sold and distributed
by Kluwer Law International,
P.O. Box 85889, 2508 CN The Hague, The Netherlands.

Library of Congress Cataloging in Publication Data is available.

ISBN (hb) 90-411-9885-7
ISBN (pb) 90-411-9886-5

Kluwer Law International incorporates the imprint
Martinus Nijhoff Publishers.

Cover © Bert Boshoff

Printed and bound in Great Britain by Antony Rowe Limited.

Foreword

At the end of the Uruguay Round of Negotiations in 1995 the more than 120 governments participating in the negotiations agreed to set up new procedures to resolve trade disputes among them by mutual agreement backed by international law and legal sanctions. For the first time in history, this process – the dispute settlement system of the World Trade Organization (WTO) – applies principles of fairness, open-dealing and mutual benefit by 'law' to trade relations between sovereign economies. Dealing with international conflict in this way helps to secure economic opportunity for billions of people as employees, entrepreneurs and consumers because it provides unique protection against unfair, arbitrary or burdensome regulations that affect international trade.

The establishment of this orderly mechanism for the settlement of disputes between Members of the WTO has been described as the "WTO's most individual contribution".

The new WTO system is at once stronger, more automatic and more credible than its GATT predecessor. This is reflected in the increased diversity of countries using it and in the tendency to resolve cases 'out of court' before they get to the final decision. The system is working as intended – as a means above all for conciliation and for encouraging resolution of disputes, rather than just for making judgements. By reducing the scope for unilateral actions, it is also an important guarantee of fair trade between smaller countries and the major trading nations.

The purpose of this Guide is to help you to understand the purpose of the system and the role it plays in the management of the international economy. We hope that this Guide will help you understand what is going on when a government takes a 'case' to the WTO and what the results of the case mean. The Guide may also help you to see how you can participate, whether as a citizen, a businessperson, a consumer, or an official in supporting your own government's role in the system or even, possibly, supporting your government in bringing or responding to a WTO case.

Peter Gallagher, a former trade negotiator and specialist in the Uruguay Round agreements has written this guide with the support of the WTO. The guide has been reviewed for accuracy by the WTO but the explanations, opinions and conclusions it presents are those of Mr. Gallagher.

Contents

Chapter Five

Chapter One
Start here

A unique experiment

This Guide is about a unique global effort to maintain peace in world trade. Just six years ago, almost all the governments of the world agreed to set up new procedures to resolve trade disputes among them by mutual agreement backed by international law and legal sanctions. For the first time in history, this process – the dispute settlement system of the World Trade Organization (WTO) – applies principles of fairness, open-dealing and mutual benefit by 'law' to trade relations between sovereign economies. Dealing with international conflict in this way helps to secure peace and economic opportunity for billions of people as employees, entrepreneurs and consumers because it provides unique protection against unfair, arbitrary or burdensome regulations that affect international trade.

The dispute settlement guarantee

'… The relevance of Article 23 [dispute settlement] obligations for individuals and the market place is particularly important since they radiate on to all substantive obligations under the WTO. If individual economic operators cannot be confident about the integrity of WTO dispute resolution and may fear unilateral measures outside the guarantees and disciplines which the [WTO] ensures, their confidence in each and every of the substantive disciplines of the system will be undermined as well.'

Panel report in *US – Section 301* (WT/DS152/R) at 7.94

The WTO is the only international body dealing with the rules of trade between nations. At its heart are the WTO Agreements, negotiated and signed by more than 140 of the world's trading nations. The Agreements are like contracts, binding governments to keep their trade regulations and policies within agreed limits so that global markets can operate as well and as fairly as possible for everyone's benefit.

The global goals of the WTO

The ultimate goal of the Organization is to improve global welfare by helping the citizens of member countries to gain the most benefit from participation in the global economy. This includes improving the economic opportunities of the poorest Member countries by helping them to access rapidly-expanding global markets, expanding their income and helping them to use their resources as effectively as possible.

Governments set out to achieve these goals more than 50 years ago when they created a system of global trade rules known as the GATT (General Agreement on Tariffs and Trade). These rules applied in exactly the same way to every Member government of GATT, from the world's richest and most powerful economy to the world's smallest and poorest economies. It was a remarkable and far-sighted agreement that brought enormous benefits to the world by helping to spur and to spread the benefits of economic growth in the second half of the 20th century.

In 1995, the rules of the GATT were extended, improved, and re-named as the rules of the World Trade Organization. But the key ideas and purposes of the WTO remained the same as they had been in GATT. As far as possible, the WTO replaces the role of 'power' in international trade relations with the rule of 'law' and with voluntary agreements based on mutual advantage between all countries. Every Member has the same 'vote' in the Organization; every member has the same entitlements; all members work together to resolve problems and establish peaceful conditions for trade. In the WTO, as a general rule, a decision is made only when every Member is ready to accept it.

There is broad agreement that the 'experiment' has been a success, so far. There has been a 'flood' of cases bought by both developed and developing countries – more than 250 cases in the first seven years – which seems to demonstrate the faith that the Members place in the system. Despite the pressures that this heavy caseload has placed on the institutions of the dispute settlement system, cases have been adjudicated in accordance with the accelerated timetable and respected independent analysts have praised the quality of the jurisprudence.

The majority of disputes notified to the WTO have been resolved without recourse to the full, compulsory adjudication process. But almost all respondent parties that have been the subject of an adverse decision by the Dispute Settlement Body (DSB) have voluntarily implemented the recommendations without the need for enforcement measures. Threats of unilateral measures by the major industrialized countries that undermined confidence in the trading system in the 1980s have disappeared. The WTO system has successfully resolved disputes between the largest economies, involving billions of dollars of trade, without bilateral conflict and without drawn-out processes that could prolong uncertainty for the commercial interests affected.

Business pressures can mean conflicts

This does not mean that there are no disagreements. Far from it! Few areas of international relations see more passion, hot tempers and bitter argument than trade and commerce.

You can probably see why disputes might arise: where business and profits are at stake, it seems there are no holds barred. Governments know, as well as business does, that sometimes in commercial deals there are 'winners and losers': if possible, 'our' winners and 'their' losers. So Governments everywhere feel the pressure to work hand-in-hand with business and with consumer or other lobby groups to ensure that their own citizens and economies are taking advantage of every opportunity.

This sort of pressure flows over into the WTO every day. In every meeting room in the WTO Headquarters you'll find officials meeting to deal with issues and disagreements that arise between Member governments because each of them is trying to help their own industries and consumers.

Keeping trade benefits in perspective

But business is only business: there are some much bigger issues at stake in world trade, as all WTO Member governments know. They understand that to achieve their goals of peaceful global growth from international trade, they can't focus only on 'winners and losers'. A broader vision is needed because, in reality, international trade agreements are very different from business deals.

Unlike business deals where each side usually seeks an advantage over the other in price, a trade deal to open markets and to maintain fair regulation and competition works because it creates winners on *both sides*. That's the key difference between the gains from trade and commercial profits: trade gains are always *mutual gains*. So although governments are, naturally, keen to ensure that their citizens profit from trade, they are aware that they cannot do this by 'gaining the upper hand' in trade regulations and policies. They know from the lessons of the great economic depression of the 1930's, and from the wars that followed, what happens when governments try to 'gain the upper hand'. And they are determined not to see that happen again.

The 'experiment'

So, there's a crucial balance to be struck by every government between helping firms and consumers in their own economies and ensuring that this 'help' doesn't reduce the gains from trade to the economy as a whole, or to the global economy in the long run. The purpose of the WTO dispute settlement system is to help governments find this balance. Disputes that are adjudicated in the WTO almost always start with some regulation intended to help a commercial interest in a member economy. If the regulation hurts the interests of other members, the Dispute Settlement system helps to restore the balance by interpreting and applying the rules of the trading system to that particular circumstance. The Member governments of the WTO don't 'punish' each other, but national regulations may have to be changed to ensure that mutual trade benefits are restored.

We've called the dispute settlement system an 'experiment' because some of its procedures – like the 'automatic' progress between stages and the binding decisions of the Dispute Settlement Body – are a new approach to international relations that has never been tried before. Also, the pressure of a large number of 'cases' right from the start, has been a tough test for the new procedures and institutions. It has been used actively, even aggressively, by a wide range of members and has helped governments to resolve some very difficult and potentially damaging disputes. So far, most Members of the WTO would say that the experiment has been successful: although they've not yet completed the 'review' of the system that they proposed to undertake at the five-year mark.

The purpose of this Guide is to help you to understand the purpose of the system and the role it plays in the management of the international economy. We hope that this Guide will help you understand what is going on when a government takes a 'case' to the WTO and what the results of the case mean. The Guide may also help you to see how you can participate, whether as a citizen, a businessperson, a consumer, or an official in supporting your own government's role in the system or even, possibly, supporting your government in bringing or responding to a WTO case.

How this Guide is organized

You may already know something about the WTO dispute settlement system: if so, you might want to look at the table of contents of the Guide and read only those parts that look like they might interest you. But if you'd like to start from the beginning, here's a 'guide to the guide' (Table 1).

What is a dispute?

A WTO dispute is a difference between two or more Member governments of the WTO where one Member claims that the actions or regulations or policies of another are damaging its interests. In most cases, disputes arise when an exporting country believes that an importing country is not treating its exported products or services fairly, in accordance with the WTO rules.

The difference becomes a WTO dispute when it is 'notified' to the WTO Secretariat by the complainant country under the provisions of one or more of the WTO Agreements. The first formal indication of a dispute is in the form of a 'request for consultations', which are confidential talks between the parties to the dispute held, normally, in Geneva. The 'request for consultations' starts a timetable of events that can lead to a ruling on the dispute by the Dispute Settlement Body (DSB) of the WTO, unless the countries concerned reach an agreement between themselves that resolves the problem.

Note that a dispute involves only governments: it's usually based on some commercial concern with the regulations of another government, but there is no WTO dispute until the government of one or other Member economy of the

Table 1: An overview of the Guide to WTO Dispute Settlement

Guide Section	Section Content	Comment
Start here	1. What is a dispute? 2. How are disputes settled? 3. An illustrated 'timetable' of dispute settlement 4. Law and democracy 5. An FAQ (short, plain language answers)	You should read this section if this is your first introduction to the WTO disputes settlement system. It contains basic information about how the disputes are resolved and how the rules of the WTO are enforced. It also shows you step-by-step how the WTO resolves disputes.
A closer look	6. The grounds for complaint 7. Mutually acceptable solutions 8. Dispute resolution – not rulemaking 9. Case-by-case approach 10. The Panel process 11. The Appeal process 13. Implementing dispute decisions 14. Developing country provisions	Here's where we get a bit more technical. This section looks at the main players in the system in more depth, detailing the different roles of the Council and Panels and the Appellate Body. We also look a little more closely at the 'legal' nature of the disputes system and at the methods used to enforce Council decisions on disputes, when necessary. Finally we look at the provisions of the DSU that apply only to developing countries.
Should you bring a complaint?	15. Has there been a breach of obligation? 16. Is there a 'non-violation' case to answer? 17. Do previous cases clarify WTO obligations? 18. Are you 'vulnerable' as a plaintiff? 19. How does intervention by other parties affect a dispute? 20. Is it realistic to expect commercial benefit or relief? 21. How long will it take? 22. How much will it cost? 23. What are the alternatives to Dispute Settlement? 24. Is 'unilateral action' an option? 25. Should you consider conciliation? 26. Is independent legal advice available? 27. Who may represent a Member?	This is what matters to you most, right? You want to know what's in it for you to get support from your government for a WTO complaint. Or may be your government is facing a complaint from another Member over a regulation that you want to preserve. Here's where we try to provide the information that will help you to evaluate your choices and to understand the choices facing Member governments. Be careful! The answers might not be as simple as you hoped.
Disputes by subject		Already, after only 5 years, the WTO has settled a wide range of disputes. You may want to review the activity so far by issue. This section provides a key to cases that have been decided under the WTO.
The 'state of play'		This section reproduces the latest information, at the time of writing, on disputes in different stages of the dispute settlement process. You can find updated information in this format on the WTO website.
Developing country experience	By the numbers Leading costs and lagging benefits? Legal assistance	The great majority of WTO members are developing countries. As a group, they were less active in dispute settlement than industrialized countries before the DSU was adopted. Now, they are much more active in pursuing their rights under the Agreements. Many developing countries still experience problems accessing the system, however.

WTO notifies the WTO Secretariat that a dispute exists. This means that, at a commercial level, the problem might already have a long history. Importing or exporting companies or investors or their agents may have had many meetings with the officials of the governments concerned. Often, there will have been exchanges – such as messages and letters or formal diplomatic notes – between the governments of the two (or more) economies over the issue. A WTO dispute exists, however, only after one or other member government decides to 'notify' the dispute.

Also, the word 'dispute' might mislead you. Don't think of a dispute as a 'trade war' or some form of a struggle between governments. It's probably more accurate, in most cases, to talk about 'resolving differences' rather than 'settling disputes'. Some of the issues certainly raise the temperature of officials and business people who are involved: after all, thousands of millions of dollars of trade can be at stake in WTO disputes such as those on the US Foreign Sales Corporations tax-subsidies or the EU ban on imports of meat that may contain artificial growth hormones. But many other disputes are simply differences that all sides are keen to resolve in an efficient, fair and friendly manner.

Technically, the grounds for a dispute under the WTO are the same as they were under Article XXIII of the General Agreement on Tariffs and Trade (GATT), which is now one of the WTO Agreements. That is, one Member alleges that another Member has done something to reduce the benefits it expects to derive from the WTO Agreements, probably – but not necessarily – in violation of the WTO rules themselves.

How are disputes settled?

Members of the WTO are encouraged to resolve their own disputes rather than have the WTO issue a ruling. The Understanding on Dispute Settlement (DSU) says that it's 'clearly preferable' to secure a 'positive solution' to the dispute that is 'mutually acceptable' to the parties and 'consistent with the covered agreements'. This is why the disputes process always begins with consultations between the Members concerned and why the process can be interrupted at any point and brought to a speedy end if the Members concerned reach a mutually acceptable solution between themselves.

If one or other of the Members in disputes asks for it, a process of 'conciliation' is also available at the time of the consultations. The Director-General of the WTO offers his 'good offices' to try to broker a settlement for Members if they request it.

If the Members involved cannot agree among themselves on the solution, then the Dispute Settlement Body (DSB) – the WTO General Council in another guise – has to make a decision about what the Agreements require. To do this, the DSB establishes a Panel of three experienced people to assess the facts of the case in the light of the provisions of the Agreements that the complainant claims are relevant to the case. The role of the Panel is to help the

DSB by making a recommendation for a decision and – possibly – a suggestion for measures that should be taken to put the situation right.

At its second meeting on the case, after the Panel report has been circulated to all WTO Members, the DSB may reject the panel's findings and recommendations but only if all the members of the Body are united in a consensus to reject the recommendation. This is unlikely to happen very often – it never *has* happened – so it's important that the recommendations are of the highest standard.

This is where the Appellate Body plays an important role (Table 2). This group of eminent legal specialists may review the Panel recommendations to ensure that they are legally sound. The Members who are parties to a dispute may ask the Appellate Body to review the Panel report and recommendations *before* the DSB takes a decision on the case. If the Appellate Body changes the recommendations of the Panel then the DSB makes its decision on the Panel report *as amended* by the Appellate Body. Only the DSB, however, has the right to make the final decision in a dispute, normally by adopting the recommendations of the Panel – as modified in some cases by the Appellate Body.

The DSB also monitors the implementation of the rulings and recommendations, and has the power to authorize 'retaliation' [suspension of concessions] when a country does not comply with a ruling within a 'reasonable period of

Table 2: Roles in the dispute settlement system

Who . . .	. . . does what?
The Dispute Settlement Body	Establishes a Panel to make recommendations on a dispute and accepts – absent a contrary consensus – the recommendations of the Panel as amended (possibly) by the Appellate Body. The only body with authority, in principle, to determine the meaning of the Agreememts.
The Panel	Temporary tribunal (3 persons) that examines the dispute and makes recommendations in light of the Agreements.
Appellate Body	A standing body of distinguished legal experts that reviews issues of law and legal reasoning in Panel reports, as requested by the Parties. May reverse unsound Panel conclusions or recommendations before they are adopted by the DSB.
Arbitrators	May be appointed by the DSB to determine a 'reasonable period of time' for the implementation of a decision.
	Under Article 25 of the DSU, parties may choose to have a dispute arbitrated as an alternative to a Panel procedure. Arbitration decisions, which parties are likely to seek only when they agree on the precise issues for resolution, must be notified to the DSB. The provisions of Articles 21 and 22 of the DSU on remedies and on the surveillance of implementation of a decision apply to Arbitral awards.
Director-General of WTO	May use his 'good offices' to assist parties to a dispute reach a 'conciliated' mutual agreement.
Experts	Assist Panels, at the request of a Panel, with advice on technical matters. A Panel may choose its own expert assistants.
WTO Secretariat	Provides administrative support to the DSB. Provides secretarial and legal assistance to the panels. May offer some impartial assistance to developing country members in the preparation of a dispute.

time'. 'Retaliation' means that the DSB authorizes the 'winner' of the case to withdraw some WTO benefits – such as reduced tariff rates – that it may have formerly extended to the 'loser'.

Three important points to note in this overview of the procedures:

1. The *process is 'automatic'* once the dispute is notified to the WTO. It can be brought to an end only by the disputants finding a mutually acceptable solution or by a decision of the DSB followed by implementation of the DSB decision.
2. There are *no 'opt outs'* for Members. Every WTO Agreement is covered by the DSU and a decision of the DSB is binding on all members, big and small, and must be implemented in accordance with a timetable that is monitored by the DSB.
3. *Most disputes are not adjudicated* by a Panel and are not decided by the DSB. Panels have been established in only about one third of all disputes notified to the WTO since January 1995. In some cases the parties notified the WTO of mutually agreed solutions and in other cases neither party wished to continue beyond the consultation phase.

How are rulings enforced?

In most cases, no special action is needed to enforce decisions of the DSB. When a Member's policies are successfully challenged, most Members inform the DSB at the meeting where the decision is taken of their intention to comply with the decision and, often, indicate when they expect to implement it.

WTO 'cases' are not intended to be contentious: there's no shame in loosing a case. There is no 'punishment' because there is no 'wrong-doing'. The outcome of a case is that the WTO Members, acting through the DSB, rule on the requirements of the Agreements as they apply in the particular circumstances of the case (Table 3). The Member who has 'lost' has not been found at fault but has been found to act in a way that reduces the benefits of the Agreement to other Members. This has to be corrected within 'a reasonable

Table 3: Case statistics (to end 2000)

Time Period	Notification of Consultations*	Panels Established*	Mutually Agreed Solutions
1995–July 1996	50	20	11
Aug 1996–July 1997	51	12	7
Aug 1997–July 1998	42	15	11
Aug 1998–July 1999	39	17	2
Aug 1999–Jan 2000	10	6	1
2000	33	12	3
Totals	**225**	**82**	**35**

* Some of these are related matters e.g. complaints by several Members on almost identical matters.

period of time' by changing the policies or regulations. The 'reasonable period of time' is frequently agreed between the 'winning' and 'loosing' members very soon after the DSB decision: or either side can ask the DSB to appoint an arbitrator to determine the 'reasonable period of time'. The maximum time allowed is normally 15 months from the date of the DSB decision.

The DSB regularly reviews progress in implementing its decisions. If the situation is not put right within the 'reasonable period of time' then the DSB may authorize the winning 'complainant' to withdraw equivalent rights and concessions from the loosing Member ('retaliation') or may require the loosing Member to pay 'compensation' – normally by giving the complainant other equivalent trade access to its markets. Compensation and retaliation are rarely authorized by the DSB. They are temporary measures that do not solve the problem that gave rise to the dispute in the first place, because they do not put the situation right. The DSU requires the loosing member to put the situation right by changing its policies or measures: offering compensation or suffering retaliation is no substitute for this.

The dispute timetable

There's a saying in most parts of the world that 'justice delayed is justice denied'. One of the strengths of the WTO disputes mechanism is that it has timetables for dealing with disputes that are designed to avoid delays (Table 4).

The 'clock' starts running on the timetable for a dispute on the day that the dispute is notified to the WTO and it runs for a total of about one year to 18 months, depending on the difficulty of the issues involved.

These approximate periods for each stage of a dispute settlement procedure are target figures – the DSU Agreement is flexible. The countries concerned can settle

Table 4: How long to settle a dispute?

Time Allowed	Process
60 days	Consultations, mediation, etc
45 days	Panel set up and panelists appointment
6 months	Final panel report to parties
3 weeks	Final panel report to WTO members
60 days	Dispute Settlement Body adopts report (if no appeal)
Total = 1 year	**(without appeal)**
60–90 days	Appeals report
30 days	Dispute Settlement Body adopts appeals report
Total = 1 y 3 m	**(with appeal)**
15 months	Time to implement (maximum without appeal) Up to 18 months (with appeal)
Total = 2 y 6 m	**(without appeal)**

their dispute themselves at any stage. Also this timetable does not take into account the time needed to prepare a dispute. Over the period since 1995 when the DSU came into effect, the average time between the DSB decision to establish a Panel and the DSB decision on the recommendation of the Panel (possibly amended by the Appellate Body) has been close to the 15-month target.

The panel process

The various stages a dispute can go through in the WTO. At all stages, countries in dispute are encouraged to consult each other in order to settle 'out of court'.

At all stages the WTO Director-General is available to offer his good offices, to mediate or to help achieve a conciliation.

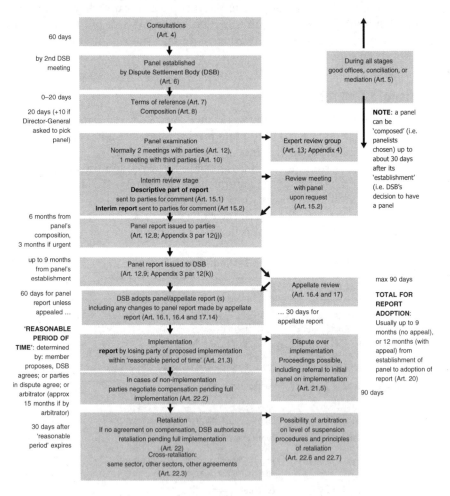

Note: Some specified times are maximums, some are minimums; some binding, some not.

The 'law' and democracy

One question comes up all the time: has the WTO become a sort of 'world trade court', imposing rigid new international 'laws' on Member governments?

You can see why people might be concerned about this. The new WTO dispute settlement system can lead 'automatically' to a decision on a dispute that a Member government will be 'forced' to accept because all WTO member economies have agreed in advance to be bound by the decisions of the DSB on disputes. Although Members can intervene in the process at several points through the DSB – and the participants in a case can bring it to an end at any time if they reach agreement – it takes a very unusual circumstance ('consensus against') to 'stop the clock' in a dispute or to reject the recommendations of the dispute Panel. It sounds like the system could be 'undemocratic' and inflexible: taking power out of the hands of elected governments and giving it to an international organization.

It's true that Members have made two 'trade-offs' in the WTO dispute settlement system that result in greater certainty, predictability and 'equity' among members but tend to reduce the detailed Member government control that was possible under the less formal GATT process.

In the first 'trade off', Members decided to accept the 'automatic' disputes process – despite the limits that it places on Members' control – in order to overcome some of the problems with the GATT system, which sometimes appeared open to 'manipulation' by interested parties.

> Members wanted the WTO system to work faster, with more predictability and fairness for all members than the former GATT system. The GATT dispute settlement on the whole worked reasonably well, but it was possible for any Member – such as the 'loser' in a case – to delay or frustrate the decision-making process. So, the 'compulsory' nature of the WTO system can be thought of as a 'democratic' device that ensures that, there are no 'opt outs'. All members, big and small, are equal partners in the Agreements and have equal rights under them; including the right to have their benefits in the Agreements protected by the dispute settlement system. The disputing Members can stop the automatic 'clock' at any time by resolving the problem for themselves. In fact, as the statistics show, it *is stopped more often than not* by the disputants deciding not to proceed with the next step of a dispute, possibly because they reached a 'mutually satisfactory conclusion'. This is the most common outcome for all of the disputes notified to the WTO so far. Finally, there is also reason to believe that Members perceived the greater certainty of the 'automatic' system to be necessary to prevent some of the largest WTO members – who had expressed dissatisfaction with the GATT system – from taking matters into their own hands.

The second 'trade-off' in the WTO dispute settlement system involved acceptance of binding 'court like' process where decisions are based on legal interpretations of the Agreements in place of the diplomatic processes which *used* to take place under GATT and which are still the origins of the Agreements themselves. This 'trade-off' adds greatly to the certainty and 'fairness' of the disputes system, although it sometimes seems to make Members subordinate to the system itself.

> The WTO dispute settlement system is unique among international tribunals for imposing judgments that Members have agreed, in advance, to accept. No other international tribunal – including the International Court of Justice (the 'World Court') – is in quite the same position. This has led to some fears that the legal decision-making process might take control away from Member governments, who are accountable to citizens, and put it in the hands of 'judges' and lawyers, who are not accountable.
>
> These fears are, however, misplaced. First, the binding nature of the decisions makes the whole WTO stronger and more effective: it means that the rules apply fairly to all, without 'opt outs' and without regard to the economic power of the parties to a dispute. Second, both the institutions of the dispute settlement system and the rules of the WTO themselves leave Members a very wide latitude to establish their own policies as long as they comply with the rules. Even when they 'lose' a case, as we will see, Member governments retain the right to determine their own policies and cannot be 'dictated to' by the WTO.
>
> Ask yourself, would governments have agreed to the 'binding' arbitration on any other terms?

In all this talk of 'legal' processes, it's important to remember that the Dispute Settlement system is not a 'court' and the rules are not 'laws' like the laws adjudicated by courts in Member countries. Although the WTO dispute settlement system is more 'court like' than the former GATT dispute settlement system the rules of the WTO are, and will remain, agreements negotiated among Member governments. In fact the DSU retains a preference for the resolution of disputes based on negotiated settlements based on 'mutual satisfaction' *not laws* in Article 3.7 (emphasis added):

> The aim of the dispute settlement mechanism is to secure **a positive solution** to a dispute. A solution **mutually acceptable to the parties** to a dispute and consistent with the covered agreements **is clearly to be preferred**.

It's clear, too, that the WTO Member governments have asserted their supreme authority in the Organization. The most 'court like' components of the system – the Panels and especially the Appellate Body – are subsidiary to the Council of Members (the DSB), unlike the courts in most Member countries, for example, which usually have constitutional independence of the 'legislative' bodies under the constitution. Members have specified – and the Appellate Body has several times noted – that only Members are able to interpret or change any of the 'laws' to which the new 'judicial' process refers. So it's more accurate to say that the binding system of arbitration in the WTO makes all members 'equal before the system' rather than subordinate to the system.

Frequently asked questions

(i) What sort of disputes does the WTO deal with?

Disputes between Member governments – more than 140 economies – over trade policies and trade-related measures covered by a WTO Agreement.

(ii) Can you give me some examples?

Here is a selection from cases that have been decided since 1995. Well over 200 disputes have been notified, covering goods trade, intellectual property, trade-related investment measures, and services trade:

- A complaint against Australian export subsidies to a company making leather car seats (Australia had to withdraw the subsidies and recover the funds paid)
- A complaint against India for failing to give the required level of protection to pharmaceutical patents (India had to change its laws)
- A complaint against the EC administration of import restrictions on poultry (the EC had to change its procedures)
- A complaint against Guatemala for not conducting adequate investigations before applying anti-dumping duties to imported cement (Guatemala had to revise its anti-dumping procedures)
- A complaint against Japan for unnecessarily restrictive quarantine procedures applied to varieties of imported fruit (Japan had to change its testing and fumigation procedures)
- A complaint against Korean safeguard measures restricting imports of dairy products (Korea had to bring its safeguard procedures into line with the WTO and GATT agreements)
- A complaint that US regulations intended to preserve rare sea-turtles were really trade restrictions on the import of shrimps (the US had to change its laws to reduce the trade impact and to make the law apply more fairly among importers).

(iii) Are all the WTO rules covered by the dispute system?

Yes. The WTO dispute settlement system covers every Agreement including the 'plurilateral' agreements on government procurement and civil aircraft, and the DSU itself.

(iv) Can businesses or citizens use the WTO dispute system?

Not directly. Only Member governments can be 'plaintiffs' or 'defendants' in a WTO case. No citizen has access to the dispute settlement system and no decisions within the system directly implicate citizens' rights. But business or citizens' interests are frequently behind the decision of a government to notify a dispute, of course.

(v) How long does it take to win a case and get a remedy through the WTO?

After two months of initial consultations, recent cases have taken an average of 13 to 16 months from the establishment of a Panel by the DSB to a decision by the DSB on the recommendation of the Panel – including a review by the Appellate Body. The 'reasonable period of time' for implementation has been set at the maximum of 15 months in several cases. So the total, in some recent cases, from first notification to the end of the implementation period has been more than 30 months. Taking into account the preparation time for a case, you should probably plan on up to three years for any moderately complex case from the time officials first begin to put the case together to the time that a successful complaint results in changes in regulations – particularly where one of the parties to the dispute is a developing country.

(vi) Is it possible to get a temporary injunction to stop some action?

No. The WTO dispute settlement system does not provide for injunctive directions to governments or for interim judgments.

(vii) Does the WTO hand out fines or other punishments?

No. The dispute settlement system is about resolving disputes between Member governments; not about 'punishment'. In most cases the only decision taken is that a Member should change its regulations or practices. Even when there is some compensation or retaliation authorized by the Dispute Settlement Body, it is equivalent to the harm caused and contains no 'punitive' measures intended to influence future behavior, for example.

(viii) How much does it cost to bring a case?

That depends a lot on the case. As a guide, it probably costs a plaintiff government and businesses in the plaintiff country several million dollars over three years (or so), if all costs are taken into account.

A Member government will probably need to dedicate one or two professional staff full time to the development and prosecution of a WTO case with the associated administrative and support costs. Senior officials and Ministers will have to be available for supervision and to make key decisions. Agencies and Ministries in the Capital whose portfolios and responsibilities may be affected by the decisions in a case will need to be consulted and there will be information costs associated with data collection – including from business, statistical sources and from foreign sources. Some Members choose to use external legal firms to assist with the preparation or review of a case, but this is not essential.

The participants in a case will need to ensure representation in Geneva (and possibly elsewhere) during the preliminary phases including the formal consultation phase. They will need to have representatives at the DSB meetings before and after the establishment of a Panel and during the decision and implementation phases of the case. They may need to have representatives appear before the Panel on two occasions and before the Appellate Body, if an appeal is made.

Businesses in the Member states will also need to consult with government agencies and may participate in the evaluation of the case or give advice to their government on the progress of implementation. Businesses will probably be called upon by a government to help with information on the facts of a case.

(ix) Are there judgments for costs against the parties?

No. Parties to a WTO dispute bear their own costs. There are no judgments as to costs. The costs of the Panelists and the Appellate Body are met from the WTO budget.

(x) Can several defendants be joined in a case?

No. The dispute settlement system is structured to handle only those disputes where there is a single respondent. There may be more than one complainant in a case and several parties may be associated with a case as interested 'third parties'. These 'third party' members have rights to provide and receive information at the Panel stage and rights to make submissions to the Appellate Body if the complainant or respondent appeal the Panel recommendations. But no assessment is made of their rights or obligations in the matter, so they are not implicated by the recommendations except to the extent that the restoration of a respondent's compliance with the Agreements may consequently benefit their interests: for example, if the respondent restores certain rights subject to MFN application. Multiple cases referring to the same matter may be referred by the DSB to a single Panel for recommendation but these are technically separate cases.

(xi) Do you need a lawyer to represent you?

No. Member governments represent themselves in the dispute settlement system as elsewhere in the WTO. The general practice in the WTO is that Members may be represented at meetings, including at meetings of the disputes Panels, by whomever they designate: so Members may include government lawyers or external advisors on their delegations.

(xii) How do I research earlier cases?

The WTO website provides full public access to reports of WTO and GATT Panels and of the WTO Appellate Body as soon as they are circulated to the Membership.

(xiii) Is there just one court at the WTO or are there several?

There are no 'courts' in the WTO although some of the institutions in the dispute settlement system are required to act in a 'court like' manner. The Member governments in Council – usually represented by their ambassadors to the WTO – form the supreme decision-making body. When it deals with disputes, the General Council is designated the Dispute Settlement Body (DSB). The DSB may appoint a Panel for each dispute to advise it on the dispute and to recommend a means of resolving the dispute. The standing Appellate Body also reports to the DSB. There is no appeal from the DSB.

(xiv) How far can you keep on appealing a decision?

Panel reports may be appealed only once and only by parties to the case. Members who are designated as interested 'third parties' by the DSB may also join in appeals.

(xv) Can we get a Panel to give us an advisory opinion?

No. Panels are established by the DSB for a specific case and have no other function than to advise on the resolution of a dispute in that case. Neither the Panel nor the Appellate Body is competent to interpret the Agreements in the abstract but only to make recommendations related to a specific case before it. The Understanding on Dispute Settlement refers Members to the decision-making processes of the covered Agreements – normally the Council established to manage the Agreement – for advice on the Agreements themselves.

(xvi) Who is responsible in my government for representing me?

This varies from government to government. Usually the agency responsible for international trade agreements (the Ministry of Foreign Affairs or the Trade Ministry) is charged with responsibility for the WTO dispute settlement system.

(xvii) Does the WTO provide legal assistance for developing countries?

Yes. Within the limits of its resources and its mandate to remain impartial, the Secretariat is directed by the Dispute Settlement Understanding to assist developing countries with e.g. the preparation of a case. Recently, the limits on the Secretariat's role have led some donors to establish a trust fund that will be used to provide more detailed and 'partial' assistance to developing countries (see the 'Advisory Centre on WTO Law', below).

Chapter Two
A closer look

The grounds for complaint

A complaint may be brought against measures that 'nullify or impair' the benefits of one or more of the WTO Agreements or measures that impede the attainment of the objectives of one of the WTO Agreements. 'Nullification' is simply the extreme case of 'impairment': the phrase means that the actions of one Member are denying wholly (or partially) the benefits of the Agreement to another.

In the majority of disputes, a member alleges – in accordance with Article XXIII.1 (a) of the GATT (1994) – that another Member has **violated** the terms of an Agreement. Such a violation, if confirmed, would amount to a '*prima facie*' case of nullification and impairment: that is, it would amount to a *presumption* of harm to the interests of the complainant or an impairment of the objectives of the Agreement. So, when the Panel finds that the complaint deals with a violation of one of the Agreements, it place the onus on the defending member to rebut the allegation.

Note that it is not necessary for a complainant Member to establish that it is actually harmed by some trade effects of the measure alleged to violate an Agreement because the *prima facie* presumption of harm applies where the measure is found to violate a rule.

The benefits of an Agreement might also be denied or reduced by a **measure that does not violate** an Agreement or by a **situation** between members that involves no 'measures' at all. These 'exotic' cases are included as grounds for complaint by Article XXIII.1 (b) and (c) of GATT (1994) and by Articles 26 (1) and (2) of the DSU. There have been several findings related to *measures* that resulted

Table 5: Grounds for complaint

Type of Ground	Description	Remedy
Violation	Measure in violation of an Agreement (Article XXIII.1 (a) of GATT)	The measure must be withdrawn
Non-violation	Measures that nullify or impair a benefit but do not violate an Agreement (Article XXIII.1 (b) of GATT)	Measure/situation may remain in place but measures should be taken to redress the 'impairment' of benefits
	Situations involving no measure that nonetheless nullify or impair a benefit (Article XXIII.1 (c) of GATT)	

in non-violation nullification and impairment under the GATT (none under the WTO, so far) but no non-violation *situation* has ever resulted in a decision of nullification and impairment.

You might wonder what business the WTO has in judging *any* dispute that does not involve a violation of the rules. It's a question that has exercised many expert commentators over the years. Probably, the inclusion of non-violation grounds for action in the 1947 text of the GATT was intended to deal with the use of non-tariff barriers that were not dealt with very successfully in the text of the GATT. If this is the case, the 'non-violation' clause could be seen as a sort of 'catch-all' that allowed the dispute settlement system to resolve trade disputes where the text of the GATT itself was deficient. But the cost of this diplomatic 'catch-all' seems to have been a certain amount of legal ambiguity.

There are two types of 'non-violation' cases in the history of the GATT dispute settlement system: those attached to claims about breaches of tariff bindings and those that are not. From 1947 to 1990, the GATT Council adopted only three 'non-violation' Panel recommendations, all of which were cases related to a tariff issue. In this form of non-violation complaint a complainant might claim that some other regulation – a measure not covered by the GATT or not in violation of GATT – had resulted in a breach of a tariff binding. For example, the United States claimed in the 1982 *Citrus* case that EC tariff preferences for Mediterranean countries, instituted after the negotiation of a bound tariff rate on imports of citrus fruit from the USA, had breached the tariff binding. Under some circumstances this sort of claim might succeed as a *violation* case (under Articles I and II of the GATT) but the USA also claimed, in the alternative, that the EC action was a non-violation case because, if the later preferential treatment of Mediterranean imports was found not to breach the binding, it nevertheless upset the 'reasonable expectations' of the United States about the value of the tariff binding at the time of negotiation (and thus nullified or impaired a benefit of the Agreement).

As you might guess, non-violation claims have to navigate some tricky ground. GATT dispute panels tried to put some scope to the claims of non-violation cases by linking the tariff-based non-violation cases to the concept of 'reasonable expectations' of the benefit of a binding. But this has to some extent compounded the ambiguity; apart from problems of finding evidence of 'reasonable expectation', the Panels could face questions such as how long should a 'reasonable expectation' of the value of a binding endure? Should the concept of 'reasonable expectation' – apparently available to WTO Panels – apply to the GATS schedules, which are constructed as 'positive lists', quite distinct from tariffs?

There have been Panel recommendations on three WTO cases, up to the end of 2000, which have involved non-violation claims: all linked to 'legitimate expectations' in the alternate to a violation claim. The first case involved Korea's implementation of its obligations under the Government Procurement Agreement (a 'plurilateral' WTO Agreement); a second case was linked to an alleged breach of 'national treatment' for imported film stock in Japan.

Neither of these non-violation claims succeeded before the Panel, although the latter Panel made an important observation about non-violation claims that indicates that they must refer – unlike violation cases – to some actual present harm to the complainant. Whereas violation claims are about *prima facie* nullification and impairment, requiring no demonstration of actual harm, non-violation claims are not linked to any such presumption of nullification and impairment with the result that the complainant must show harm exists. See the panel report in WT/DS44/R at 10.57.

Only in the third case (India – Patent protection for pharmaceutical and agricultural chemical products (WT/DS50)) did the Panel make an affirmative finding on non-violation nullification or impairment. This case concerned the expectations of the United States concerning the competitive position of its firms in the Indian marketplace following India's implementation of the Agreement on Trade-Related Aspects of Intellectual Property Rights (TRIPS).

The Appellate Body report in the *India-Patent Protection* case reversed the Panel's positive finding on the non-violation claim, however, citing confused reasoning in dealing with the concept of 'reasonable expectations'. It acknowledged that the reasoning of the GATT Panels on this point is available to WTO Panels as guidance. But the Appellate Body report constructs further strict limits around this terminology by reference to the Vienna Convention on the Interpretation of Treaties:

> The legitimate expectations of the parties to a treaty are reflected in the language of the treaty itself. The duty of a treaty interpreter is to examine the words of the treaty to determine the intentions of the parties. This should be done in accordance with the principles of treaty interpretation set out in Article 31 of the *Vienna Convention.*
>
> WT/DS50/AB/R para 45

Mutually agreed solutions

The DSU states (Section 3.7) the preference of Members for a resolution of disputes based on 'mutually agreed solutions' that are consistent with the covered agreements rather than on Panel recommendations. This preference reminds us that the system is built on agreements between member governments and not on an abstract code of 'laws'. The preferred outcome is not the determination of whether one side or the other is in breach of an Agreement but the resolution of the problem on (almost) any basis that the disputants can agree.

Disputants normally arrive at mutually agreed solutions during bilateral discussions – possibly as part of the 'consultation' process. Mutual agreement is possible at any time up to the circulation of a panel report. You might imagine that the 'respondent' in most disputes would try very hard to put the matter to rest through 'mutual agreement' at the consultation phase or, in any case, before the Panel report is issued. In practice, however, some members seem ready to 'take their chances' with a Panel. A mutually agreed solution may be delayed during the formal 'consultations' because the disputants wait to see the strength of the other side's 'case' before a Panel before they seriously consider settlement on a bilateral basis. Mutual agreement also becomes less likely the further a panel process proceeds as parties become entrenched in a legal struggle that – perhaps goaded by the media – governments feel compelled to 'win'. A few disputes have however been settled by mutual agreement after an interim Panel report was circulated – when the outcome seemed to be clear:

- In EC – Butter (WT/DS72), the parties reached a mutually agreed solution after the Panel had submitted its final report.
- In EC – Scallops (Request by Canada, WT/DS7) the mutually agreed solution was reached after the Panel had issued the Interim report.
- In U.S.A. – DRAM Semiconductors (WT/DS99), the parties reached agreement at the stage of the proceedings under Article 21.5 of the DSU, after the Compliance Panel had issued its Interim report.

There are *some* legal conditions that the DSU attaches to mutually agreed solutions. Under the provisions of sections 3.5 and 3.6 of the DSU, they must be notified to the DSB; they must be consistent with the WTO Agreements; must not nullify or impair benefits accruing to any Member under the Agreements, nor impede the attainment of any objective of those Agreements.

Why does the DSU express a preference for dispute resolution by 'mutual agreement'? The Understanding does not spell out its reasons; it is content to say that the reasons are 'clear' ('clearly to be preferred'). Perhaps this indicates that we should look for inchoate motives: shared experiences of Members such as the history of the dispute settlement system or the 'culture' of the WTO. What is 'clear' is that mutually agreed solutions are particularly compatible with the 'diplomatic' character of the trade agreements in the GATT and – to a lesser extent – in the WTO. The GATT and the GATT dispute settlement system is said to have had a 'diplomatic' character – often contrasted with the more legalistic character of the WTO, particularly the DSU.

The problem with 'diplomatic' agreements

'Diplomatic' agreements are sufficient to represent an understanding between the parties engaged in the agreement, but they are not necessarily drafted with tight, legal precision. They might contain ambiguous language reflecting compromises that satisfy the parties but that might be open to unintended interpretation if subjected to rigorous analysis or analysis outside the context in which it was drafted. This means 'diplomatic' agreements may not be robust if circumstances change or if more countries seek to adhere to the agreement.

Although these problems have been among the reasons that Members have moved in the direction of more 'legalistic' WTO Agreements and procedures, the choice of the 'diplomatic' approach to agreements is nevertheless practical in some circumstances. Diplomatic agreements can be reached relatively quickly once the parties are ready to 'deal'; also, what they lack in forensic precision may be compensated by language which expresses aspects of the relationship in a way that the parties find satisfying and which helps to heal a breach in a relationship.

We could speculate that the preference expressed in the DSU relates to the practical advantages of a 'diplomatic' solution to a bilateral dispute:

• Quick to conclude: once the parties are willing;
• Low cost: much less for the parties and for the WTO itself than pursuing a full Panel-plus-Appeal process;
• Sufficiently robust for a purely bilateral matter: third parties will be interested but have no need to adhere to the agreement;
• Less contentious: because more 'private'.

The preference also seems to reflect an intention on the part of the drafters of the DSU to avoid a purely 'legal' system of dispute settlement. In such a system, 'mutual agreement' would not be the 'preferred' outcome: rather the preferred outcome for every case would probably be an adjudication that contributed to the overall 'jurisprudence'.

Why might the disputants want to reach a 'mutually agreed' solution? The lower costs are likely to be a significant motive – although many 'plaintiff' parties may already have invested significant resources in the preparation of a dispute. But questions of 'face' are probably even more important. A 'mutually agreed' solution has a smaller impact on the credibility of 'loser's' policies than an imposed solution: it implies that concessions may have been made by both sides to achieve a solution. This avoids the – unintended but inevitable – perception of a foreign policy reversal when a solution is imposed by the DSU on the 'loser' in a case that is adjudicated by a Panel.

Are 'mutually agreed solutions' the only alternative outcome to a decision by the DSU? No: it seems not. A surprising implication of the statistics on WTO disputes is that the majority of disputes are *neither* decided by a Panel nor are they the subject of a 'mutually agreed solution' that is notified to the DSU. For example, as of July 2000 there had been 225 disputes notified, but only 120 resolved by Panels or 'mutual agreement'. So what happens in the other cases?

At any one time, the number of 'disputes notified' includes many cases that will, in due course, proceed to either a 'mutually agreed' or adjudicated solution. But because the number of cases is growing quickly, there are apparently many more notified cases waiting for the next step in the dispute settlement system process than cases either 'mutually agreed' or resolved by a Panel recommendation, so far. Also, some cases just seem to disappear after notification without either side requesting the establishment of a Panel or notifying a 'mutually agreed' solution. Perhaps circumstances change so that the dispute goes away – for example, the underlying commercial issues might be resolved – or perhaps one side or the other *unilaterally* takes steps that eliminate the dispute. Whatever the reason, the WTO has no authority to investigate the outcome of the notified dispute and no interest in doing so if the parties are content to let the matter 'fall off' the schedule of disputes.

If a mutually agreed solution is notified before the final report of the Panel is ready, no further dispute processes are undertaken. The Panel confines its report to a brief description of the case and a report that a solution has been found (Article 12.7 of the DSU). The disputants notify the relevant Agreements councils and committees of the mutual agreement 'where any member may raise any point relating thereto' (DSU section 3.6). This formulation does not explicitly appear to give the Members the right to object to, or seek to modify any notified solution. But, of course, every Member retains the right to begin dispute proceedings with respect to any measure – including a measure that forms part of a 'mutually agreed solution' – if they consider that it impairs their benefits under the Agreement or the achievement of the objectives of the Agreement.

As with all dispute settlement outcomes, mutually agreed solutions do not bind other members and do not imply an interpretation of the Agreements. Unlike 'imposed' outcomes, however, they are not subject to the reviews of implementation of cases by the DSB.

There is a second type of 'mutually agreed' solution that can occur after the DSB decision: an agreement on implementation. If the DSB finds that there has been a violation of an Agreement, then the DSU requires that Panels recommend the restoration of compliance with the Agreement(s). But the disputants may reach agreement between them on the 'reasonable period of time' for implementation and on other details that resolve their dispute: avoiding the intervention of arbitrators or decisions by the DSB on the rectification of the dispute. Any such mutual agreement should be reported to the DSB.

Dispute Resolution – not rulemaking

It's very important to understand that the intent of the dispute settlement system is to resolve disputes, not to interpret the rules of the WTO in a way that makes new rules or adds to existing rules. At most, the dispute settlement system 'clarifies' existing WTO rules.

The duty of the dispute Panels is to assist the DSB to resolve the dispute:

> … Accordingly, a panel should make an objective assessment of the matter before it, including an objective assessment of the facts of the case and the applicability of and conformity with the relevant covered agreements, and make such other findings as will assist the DSB in making the recommendations or in giving the rulings provided for in the covered agreements. Panels should consult regularly with the parties to the dispute and give them adequate opportunity to develop a mutually satisfactory solution.

The components of the Panel's forensic task, therefore, are:

- To make an objective assessment of the facts of the case;
- To assess the applicability of certain provisions of the relevant agreements to the case;
- To assess conformity of measures cited in the complaint with the cited provisions of the relevant agreements;
- To make other findings that will assist the DSB in making recommendations or rulings in accordance with the provisions of the covered agreements.

The task of the Appellate Body is still more limited:

> … The Appellate Body shall hear appeals from panel cases. … an appeal shall be limited to issues of law covered in the panel report and legal interpretations developed by the panel.
>
> Article 17.1 and 17.6 of the DSU

When the Panel's work is done, and any appeal is heard, the DSU obliges the Panel to make a recommendation. Where it finds that a measure is inconsistent with a covered Agreement:

> … it shall recommend that the Member concerned bring the measure into conformity with that agreement.
>
> Article 19 of the DSU

The Panel or Appellate Body may, in addition, make suggestions about implementation:

> In addition to its recommendations, the panel or Appellate Body may suggest ways in which the Member concerned could implement the recommendations.
>
> Article 19 of the DSU

In practice, almost all Panels have limited themselves to recommendations that the 'losing' member restore compliance with the Agreement(s).

Although none of these provisions seem to allow much room for 'creative' input by the Panels or the members of the Appellate Body, the report of any Panel or Appellate Body clearly shows the members engaged in interpreting the Agreements in the light of the facts of the case. You might expect the interpretations to make room for original contributions to the body of WTO 'case law' and to comprise, in fact if not in law, a body of precedents – similar to those that are created by courts in countries that are part of the common law tradition – that would apply in future disputes and would influence decisions by future Panels and even Member Governments in their relations with each other.

Neither the Panels nor the Appellate Body has any definitive or precedent-making role. It is important not to assume that because they behave in many senses like other tribunals that operate in domestic legal systems, the Panel and Appellate Body reports have the same 'creative' effect as the judgments of domestic courts. Although understandable, such assumptions about the WTO dispute settlement system are simply not consistent with the rules and practices as specified in the Agreements.

We have seen that the functions of the Panels and the Appellate body are defined in such a way as to limit their 'creative' input in interpreting or adding to the rights or obligations of Members. In addition, the WTO Council (or Ministerial Council) specifically reserves for itself the right to adopt any interpretation of a WTO Agreement that could implicate rights or obligations. The Agreement Establishing the WTO is very specific on this point.

> The Ministerial Conference and the General Council shall have the exclusive authority to adopt interpretations of this Agreement and of the Multilateral Trade Agreements. In the case of an interpretation of a Multilateral Trade Agreement in Annex 1, they shall exercise their authority on the basis of a recommendation by the Council overseeing the functioning of that Agreement. The decision to adopt an interpretation shall be taken by a three-fourths majority of the Members.
>
> Article IX.2

This means that the recommendations of Panels and the reports of the Appellate Body do not comprise 'interpretations of the Agreements', *even* when adopted in the normal way by the DSB – which is the WTO Council in another guise.

This point about who is authorized to make an 'interpretation' of the Agreements and what that means isn't easy to understand; but it's crucial for understanding the relationship between the dispute system and the Agreements. Under WTO rules, contained in the *Agreement Establishing the WTO*, an interpretation of the Agreements requires, at a minimum, an intention to interpret the Agreement concerned **plus** a two-thirds majority decision in the Council. Neither of these is present in the normal course of a decision by the DSU on a dispute Panel recommendation.

- The decision of the DSB is made on a recommendation from a Panel to require, for example, that the respondent in a *violation* dispute comply with the Agreement(s). It's not a recommendation to interpret the Agreements, as we have seen, because neither the Panel or the Appellate Body may properly make such a recommendation.
- The decision of the DSB on the recommendation of a Panel is taken in accordance with Article 2.4 of the DSU: that is, by consensus not by a two-thirds (or greater) majority as required for a change in the provisions of the Agreement(s).

But, you ask, don't the decisions *effectively* interpret the Agreements simply by endorsing one side or the other of a dispute under an Agreement? The answer is 'no'; the recommendations only *'clarify'* the provisions of the Agreement(s) as they apply to a specific case, without modifying the rights or obligations of members. The DSU itself makes this point in some detail:

> The dispute settlement system of the WTO is a central element in providing security and predictability to the multilateral trading system. The Members recognize that it **serves to preserve the rights and obligations of Members** under the covered agreements, **and to clarify the existing provisions of those agreements** in accordance with customary rules of interpretation of public international law. Recommendations and rulings of the DSB cannot add to or diminish the rights and obligations provided in the covered agreements.
>
> *Article 3.2*

The Appellate Body has identified the 'customary rules of interpretation of international law', that are to be used in clarifying the existing provisions of the Agreements as we'll see later. But these interpretive practices aren't intended to lead to new WTO rights or obligations: the interpretations can be no more than 'clarifications'. After all, as the DSU says, the system is intended to 'preserve the rights and obligations of Members' meaning that the recommendations of the DSB 'cannot add to or diminish' those rights and obligations.

The case-by-case approach

'Ok,' you say, 'but isn't this distinction between an 'interpretation' that might alter the rights and obligations of Members and a 'clarification' that does not alter those rights and obligations a lot like 'splitting hairs'? Isn't it a very fine distinction? Is it really 'watertight?''

It is a fine distinction and some respected commentators on the WTO argue that it is not completely satisfactory. They say that it allows Panels and the Appellate Body to make *authoritative*, if not *legislated* 'law' – the decisions that we call 'clarifications' – much more quickly and much more frequently than the WTO Members can ever hope to do for themselves. After all, they say, Members

in Council have to follow the laborious qualified-majority procedure to make official interpretations and would probably be able to make these changes only at
meetings of the Ministerial Council – which normally meets once every two years.

In response to these claims, let's admit that an 'authoritative clarification',
even if it's tied to a specific set of circumstances that is not intended to have any
consequences for the rights and obligations of Members, *nevertheless* has the
potential to change the way in which Members view the value of rights and
obligations in analogous circumstances. But notice that this does *not* give the
statement the force of a rule or a 'law'.

If a Panel or the Appellate Body finds, for example, that in order to comply
with the provisions of the WTO Agreement on Safeguards, it is necessary to
demonstrate that the threat from imports affected by a safeguard measure was,
in fact, unforeseen – as required by Article XIX of GATT on Safeguards but not
explicitly by the WTO Agreement – then Members perceptions of their rights
and obligations with respect to safeguard action in future under the WTO
Agreement may well have been altered. Yet this reasoning, which founded a recommendation in the case (WT/DS121 Argentine Footwear – a case bought by
the EC), is only a clarification of the way in which the Agreement on Safeguards
applied to a specific safeguard action by Argentina. Although an 'authoritative'
statement, it is *not* a new rule on Safeguards and does *not* add anything to the
Agreement on Safeguards or to Article XIX of GATT.

The Appellate Body, in its report on Japan – Taxes on Alcoholic Beverages
acknowledged the subtle power of GATT Panel reports (and by extension,
WTO Panel reports) to alter the 'legitimate expectations' of Members. The
Appellate Body said, '... adopted panel reports are an important part of the
GATT *acquis* ['legacy']. They are often considered by subsequent panels. They
create legitimate expectations among WTO Members, and, therefore, should be
taken into account where they are relevant to any dispute.' (WT/DS8/AB/R –
section E). But the Appellate Body added, 'However, they are not binding,
except with respect to resolving the particular dispute between the parties to
that dispute. In short, their character and their legal status have not been
changed by the coming into force of the WTO Agreement.'

The conclusion that the Appellate Body drew from this reasoning was that even
adopted Panel Reports did not comprise a standard by which the Agreements
must subsequently be interpreted. They did not, in other words, have any role as
binding precedent. This view was confirmed, said the Appellate Body, by the
assertion – that we saw earlier – of the exclusive role of the Council in making any
interpretation of the Agreements that could alter rights and obligations of
Members. The Appellate Body agreed with the Panel, in this case, however, that
the reasoning in any earlier Panel reports, including those GATT Panel reports
that were not adopted, might contain useful guidance for subsequent Panels.

So the distinction between 'interpretations' and 'clarifications' is authorized by
the Agreements and confirmed by the reports of the Appellate Body. It remains
a point of debate among commentators, however, and may be one of those

matters that will become clearer in practice. A lot of national constitutions contain similar fine distinctions in the 'separation of powers' that are only clarified by practice, in the end. As we will see when we look at the work of the Appellate Body, it has been particularly careful to acknowledge Members' rights to make interpretations of the Agreements and to give Members a wide latitude of choice when determining whether particular policies conform to the Agreements.

The Panel Process

> 'Our function in this case is judicial'
> *Panel report in US – Section 301 (WT/DS152/R at 7.12)*

When consultations fail to resolve a dispute – as they frequently do – the disputant bringing the complaint may request the DSB in writing to establish a Panel to make recommendations on the compulsory resolution of the dispute. The role of the Panel is to make an 'objective assessment of the matter before it' by reviewing the facts and legal arguments submitted by the parties to the dispute, and by making findings on the consistency of a Member's measures with the WTO Agreements (Article 11 of the DSU).

(i) Who may serve on a Panel?

A new panel is formed for each dispute. Panels usually comprise three individuals with relevant trade policy, law or economics experience, who are selected by the parties to examine the particular dispute. The Panelists serve in their personal capacity and may not be nationals of the countries involved in the dispute unless the disputants agree otherwise. The DSU takes the trouble to characterize potential Panelists as:

> ... well-qualified governmental and/or non-governmental individuals, including persons who have served on or presented a case to a panel, served as a representative of a Member or of a contracting party to GATT 1947 or as a representative to the Council or Committee of any covered agreement or its predecessor agreement, or in the Secretariat, taught or published on international trade law or policy, or served as a senior trade policy official of a Member.
>
> Article 8 of the DSU

In other words, people from 'inside' the trade policy milieu – although, the DSU also stipulates that the members of a particular Panel should also have 'a sufficiently diverse background and a wide spectrum of experience'.

Nominations for each Panel are drawn by the Secretariat from a 'roster' of names, and qualifications, contributed by Members. Disputants may object to individual nominees for 'compelling reasons' but if there is no agreement on the composition of the Panel within 20 days then the Director-General of the WTO, with the advice of the Chairman of the DSB and the Chairman of the Committee of the relevant Agreement or Council may decide who should be on the Panel.

(ii) What must Panels consider?

What does a Panel have to consider in order to make an 'objective assessment of the matter before it'? Briefly, a Panel must determine the facts of the case described in its terms of reference and, after considering the arguments and rebuttals of the parties to the dispute, must evaluate these facts in the light of the covered Agreements and make a recommendation. A panel need not consider every matter in a case: it need only make the decisions it considers necessary to resolve the dispute.

Panels appear to be tribunals in the 'adversarial' tradition of the common-law system because they meet to hear and evaluate the arguments of the parties to the dispute including the initial submissions and rebuttals of each side as to the facts of the case and the alleged breaches of the Agreements. But the Panels also have broad authority to investigate the facts of the case for themselves, in the traditions of the 'first instance' tribunals in civil-law countries. They need not establish all of the facts 'de novo', the Appellate Body has ruled in its report on EC Hormones (WT/DS48/AB/R at 117), but neither must they adopt an attitude of 'total deference' to the parties.

The Appellate Body has confirmed that Panels have virtually unfettered discretion to seek information and advice and the Parties to the dispute have a legal obligation to respond fully to Panel requests for information. In its report on United States – Shrimp ('Shrimp-Turtle') the Appellate Body stated

> It is particularly within the province and the authority of a panel to determine the need for information and advice in a specific case, to ascertain the acceptability and relevancy of information or advice received, and to decide what weight to ascribe to that information or advice or to conclude that no weight at all should be given to what has been received.
>
> ...
>
> The thrust of Articles 12 and 13, taken together, is that the DSU accords to a panel established by the DSB, and engaged in a dispute settlement proceeding, ample and extensive authority to undertake and to control the process by which it informs itself both of the relevant facts of the dispute and of the legal norms and principles applicable to such facts. That authority, and the breadth thereof, is indispensably necessary to enable a panel to discharge its duty imposed by Article 11 of the DSU to 'make an objective assessment of the matter before it, including an objective assessment of the facts of the case and the applicability of and conformity with the relevant covered agreements ...'

WT/DS58/AB/R, paras.104 and 106

In *Canada – Measures Affecting the Export of Civilian Aircraft* (WT/DS70/ AB/R) the Appellate Body said that the word 'should' in Article 13 must be taken as an obligation on Members to respond to a Panel's request for information, not as an exhortation:

> A Member *should* respond promptly and fully to any request by a panel for such information as the panel considers necessary and appropriate.
>
> Article 13 of the DSU, emphasis added

If there were any doubt about the legal obligation on members to provide full information to the Panel, says the Appellate Body, then the 'right to seek information' conferred on the Panel by Article 13 would be meaningless. In practice, Panels usually rely on the disputants to supply the facts of the case – which they verify by providing the factual part of their report to the parties for comment at an early stage.

Of course, Panels do not have powers to compel the parties to give evidence: this is a dispute settlement between sovereigns, after all. Where a Panel is unable to elicit the cooperation of Parties to a dispute in providing information, it may choose to draw 'adverse inferences' from the refusal: that is, they may decide that the Party refusing to provide the information had 'something to hide'.

Panels may accept evidence in confidence from the Parties and protect its further disclosure. This procedure is becoming more common as Panels seek confidential commercial information in order to make assessments about the existence of a subsidy, for example. The Appellate Body has confirmed on a number of occasions that all information submitted to a Panel by a Party to a dispute – other than non-confidential summaries – and all deliberations of the Panel must be treated as confidential. This is the intention of Article 18.2 of the DSU and para. 3 of Annex 3 ('Working Procedures'). Special procedures may be adopted by each Panel and by the Appellate Body to further protect 'confidential business information', including stipulations that any documents be returned to the Party providing them and all copies be destroyed at the conclusion of a case.

Finally, a Panel need not consider every allegation made by the complainant or every argument offered in rebuttal. The Appellate Body – which has encouraged Panels to exercise 'judicial economy' in their work – has declared that a Panel need address only those claims which must be addressed in order to resolve the matter in issue in the dispute (United States – Shirts and Blouses, WT/DS33/AB/R, p. 19). This means, said the Appellate Body, that a panel has the discretion to determine the claims it must address in order to resolve the dispute between the parties – *provided* that those claims are within that panel's terms of reference.

(iii) Request for a panel

The complainant's request for a panel will result in the establishment of a Panel unless there is a consensus not to form a Panel. This is so unlikely that it is probably safe to say that the establishment of a Panel is 'inevitable.' But the complainant must be careful in composing its request to be complete, or its case may not succeed.

What does a complainant have to include in its written request for the establishment of a Panel? The requirements are indicated in DSU Article 6.2 which says that the request:

> ... shall indicate whether consultations were held, identify the specific measures at issue and provide a brief summary of the legal basis of the complaint sufficient to present the problem clearly. In case the applicant requests the establishment of a panel with other than standard terms of reference, the written request shall include the proposed text of special terms of reference.

In several WTO cases the respondents have tried to avail themselves of a 'procedural' defence, asking the Appellate Body to reverse the finding on the basis that the request for the Panel was not in the right form. The response of the Appellate Body to this legal 'tactic' has been to emphasize that what is required – in line with the overall expectation that the parties will deal with each other in 'good faith' – is *fairness*. The request must be made in a form that allows the respondent to know precisely what is being claimed.

The Appellate Body has made several attempts to clarify the requirements of the DSU on the form of the request. The most important rulings are found in its reports on *EC – Bananas* (WT/DS27) and in *Korea – Safeguards on Dairy* (WT/DS98). In those reports the Appellate Body says that the complainant does not have to detail its case in the request: but it must set out all of its claims using *at a minimum* a list of references to the articles of the covered Agreements that are alleged to have been breached. In some cases, however, a 'mere listing' of the Articles may not be enough to indicate what legal claims the complainant is making. The level of detail required depends on the information needed to give the respondent a fair opportunity to prepare a defence.

> ... whether the mere listing of the articles claimed to have been violated meets the standard of Article 6.2 must be examined on a case-by-case basis. In resolving that question, we take into account whether the ability of the respondent to defend itself was prejudiced, given the actual course of the panel proceedings, by the fact that the panel request simply listed the provisions claimed to have been violated.
>
> WT/DS98/AB/R at 127

The Appellate Body also distinguishes between the *claims* that must be set out in a request for a Panel – and provide the basis for a panel's terms of reference – and the *arguments* that support and detail the claims. Here is what the Appellate Body said:

> [In the EC- Bananas case] it was sufficient for the Complaining Parties to list the provisions of the specific agreements alleged to have been violated without setting out detailed arguments as to which specific aspects of the measures at issue relate to which specific provisions of those agreements.

In our view, there is a significant difference between the *claims* identified in the request for the establishment of a panel, which establish the panel's terms of reference under Article 7 of the DSU, and the *arguments* supporting those claims, which are set out and progressively clarified in the first written submissions, the rebuttal submissions and the first and second panel meetings with the parties.

WT/DS27/AB/R at 141

Claims that are not specific – and therefore not reflected specifically in the terms of reference for the Panel – will fail. In *India – Pharmaceutical Patents* (WT/DB50/AB/R) the United States used an inclusive formula – 'including but not necessarily limited to' – when referring to provisions of the TRIPS Agreement that it believed were violated by India's measures. The Appellate Body ruled that this formulation was insufficiently specific to allow the Panel to consider a matter under an article that had not specifically been named in the US request or the terms of reference of the Panel. Furthermore, the Appellate Body rejected the Panel's proposal to allow the United States in that case to amend its claim during arguments before the Panel.

Parties must be forthcoming and open with each other at all stages of the disputes process, the Appellate Body says, to ensure that the DSU requirement of 'good faith' is met:

All parties engaged in dispute settlement under the DSU must be fully forthcoming from the very beginning both as to the claims involved in a dispute and as to the facts relating to those claims. Claims must be stated clearly. Facts must be disclosed freely. This must be so in consultations as well as in the more formal setting of panel proceedings. In fact, the demands of due process that are implicit in the DSU make this especially necessary during consultations. For the claims that are made and the facts that are established during consultations do much to shape the substance and the scope of subsequent panel proceedings. If, in the aftermath of consultations, any party believes that all the pertinent facts relating to a claim are, for any reason, not before the panel, then that party should ask the panel in that case to engage in additional fact-finding. But this additional fact-finding cannot alter the claims that are before the panel – because it cannot alter the panel's terms of reference.

India – Pharmaceutical Patents WT/DB50/AB/R at 94

(iv) Terms of reference

The Panel's terms of reference are important because they

- give the respondent and third parties sufficient information concerning the claims to allow them to prepare a case
- 'establish the jurisdiction of the Panel by defining the precise claims at issue in the dispute' (Brazil – Desiccated Coconut WT/DS22/AB/R at 22).

The Appellate Body has repeatedly stated that a panel may consider *only* those claims it has the authority to consider under its Terms of Reference – which are adopted by the DSB based on the written request from the complainant made toward the end of the consultation period. In its report on India – Patents on Pharmaceutical Products (WT/DS50/AB/R at 92) the Appellate Body criticized the decision of the Panel to consider *any* claim made prior to the end of the Panel meeting. The Appellate Body said that although a Panel has some discretion in establishing its own working procedures, this discretion does not extend to usurping the role of the DSB by, as in this case, agreeing to extend the terms of reference provided by the DSB under Art 7 of the Understanding.

(v) Burden of proof

In the cases brought so far under the WTO dispute settlement system, there have been several debates about the 'burden of proof'. The Appellate Body has applied the procedure that it says is

> ... a generally accepted cannon of evidence in civil law, common law and in fact, of most jurisdictions, that the burden of proof rests upon the party, whether complainant or defending, who asserts the affirmative of a particular claim or defence
>
> United States Woven Blouses and Shirts – WT/DS33/AB/R at 14

Parties – and even Panels – are sometimes confused about the 'burden of proof' when the complainant is alleging violation of the terms of an Agreement – and therefore '*prima facie* nullification and impairment.' Even where a *prima facie* violation of an agreement is alleged, the complainant is under an obligation ('burden of proof') to demonstrate that the facts support its allegations. Only *after* the fact of the inconsistency of a measure with the Agreement(s) is established does the 'burden of proof' shift to the respondent. At that stage, the *prima facie* presumption of nullification and impairment 'in the absence of effective refutation by the defending party, requires a panel, as a matter of law, to rule in favour of the complaining party presenting the *prima facie* case' (Appellate Body report on EC Hormones – WT/DS48/AB/R at 104).

(vi) Are there ethical standards for Panels?

The 'Rules of Conduct' for disputes adopted by the DSB in 1996 sets standards of behavior for every one serving

- on a Panel
- in the Appellate Body
- as an Arbitrator determining the 'reasonable period of time' for implementation
- as an expert advising a Panel.

The Rules also cover any person who holds a role as a chairman of one of the covered Agreements during the course of a dispute, and members of the WTO Secretariat.

In summary, the rules apply a 'governing principle' to the conduct of these persons that explicitly requires them to act with the highest professional and ethical standards in connection with a dispute:

> Each person covered by these Rules … shall be independent and impartial, shall avoid direct or indirect conflicts of interest and shall respect the confidentiality of proceedings of bodies pursuant to the dispute settlement mechanism.

WT/DSB/RC/1

(vii) What processes does a Panel follow?

Panels have detailed working procedures set out in Annex 3 to the DSU. The Working Procedures provide among other things for:

Confidential panel processes The members of the Panel meet in private meetings among themselves and in 'closed-door' meetings with the parties. The parties meet with the Panel only at the latter's invitation. No formal records are taken of these meetings.

Two sets of written submissions from the parties (first written submissions and rebuttal submissions). Written submissions are the primary means of persuading the panel. These present the facts of the case and the legal arguments relating to the specific trade rules alleged to have been breached, usually in exhaustive detail. 'Oral' statements made at the panel meetings are in fact written and provided to the panel and other parties prior to delivery.

Two substantive meetings are held with the parties, including a third party session. Although practice varies between panels, questions from the panel are often provided in writing, and written responses generally permitted, particularly on questions of a technical nature. Questions from one party to the other are put through the panel. Witnesses are not required and are never called by any party to a dispute.

Panel decision-making is not addressed in the DSU. Panels are permitted to determine for themselves how they will arrive at the views reported in their reports and the recommendations that they make. Under the GATT there were a number of dissenting reports from individual Panelists. In WTO cases so far there has only been one minor dissent recorded in a panel report (WT/DS165/R concerning US measures taken in retaliation against the EC).

A panel should aim to issue its report within six months, or within three months in cases of urgency. But, in practice, it is not uncommon for panel reports to be delayed beyond the six-month time period where the subject matter involves complex technical or scientific issues such as under the Sanitary and Phytosanitary Agreement or where the parties themselves seek delays. Where the dispute concerns the Agreement on Subsidies and Countervailing Measures on disputes involving prohibited and actionable subsidies there is an accelerated set of procedures.

The main stages of a dispute (please also see the illustrated timetable) are:

1. Each party to the dispute transmits to the panel its written submission on the facts and arguments in the case, in advance of the first substantive meeting of the Panel. At that first meeting, the complainant presents its case and the responding party its defence. Third parties that notified their interest in the dispute may also present their views at the first substantive meeting. Formal rebuttals are made at the second substantive meeting.
2. In cases where a party raises scientific or other technical matters, the panel may appoint an expert review group to provide an advisory report.
3. The panel submits descriptive (factual and argument) sections of its report to the parties, giving them two weeks to comment. After taking any comments on the facts into account, the panel then submits an interim report, including its findings and conclusions, to the parties, giving them one week to request a review. The period of review is not to exceed two weeks, during which the panel may hold additional meetings with the parties.
4. A final report is submitted to the parties and three weeks later, it is circulated to all WTO members.
5. If the panel decides that the measure in question is inconsistent with the terms of the relevant WTO Agreement, the panel recommends that the member concerned bring the measure into conformity with that agreement. It may also suggest ways in which the member could implement the recommendation.

Panel reports are adopted by the DSB within 60 days of circulation, unless one party notifies its decision to appeal or a consensus emerges in the DSB against the adoption of the report (has never happened).

(viii) Who may appear before a Panel?

The short answer is: any person delegated by a Member government to represent it before a Panel may do so. This includes government officials, private lawyers and even members of 'civil society', such as business people, representatives of NGOs and lobbyists. However, no person who is not a member of the delegation of one of the Parties to the dispute – or a WTO official – may attend a Panel meeting – for example as an 'observer' – let alone represent a government before a panel. This bar on attendance has attracted a criticism from commentators who think that the WTO, in general, and the dispute settlement system in particular, should be more 'open'.

The reason that Panel meetings are not 'open' to the public is that Member governments do not want them to be. The Working Procedures annexed to the DSU impose this rule and the Members may change it in the future if they wish. Some commentators argue that it would help to improve 'civil society's' understanding of the WTO if the Panel hearings were open. This may be so: but there is no reason to think that open panel hearings would improve the function of the system.

Panel meetings are not like 'court' hearings in a democratic state where constitutional legitimacy requires that the courts operate in a manner where justice is 'seen to be done'.

Firstly, no popular constitution underlies the WTO; it's a forum embodying agreements among sovereign governments, not a body created by citizens. The legitimacy of the dispute settlement system lies in Members' acceptance of the DSU, not in constitutional ideas such as 'justice' or 'democratic legitimacy' (important though those concepts are).

Secondly, Panel meetings with the parties do not have the same impact on the Panel's recommendations as, for example, a court hearing has on a verdict. The opportunity for oral presentations, argument and rebuttal is not as important in a case as the precision of the claims and the written presentation and analysis of the facts in the parties' written submissions. Observing the Panel's work in the hearings would not add much to outside understanding of the case.

Thirdly, Panels and those that appear before them have well-defined 'Rules of Conduct' that guide their actions, particularly when it comes to confidential information. It would be impractical to seek to apply these same rules to observers and it is not clear that the demand for 'openness' would be satisfied if the Panel meetings were open only for limited public statements.

(ix) Expert assistance

Article 13.2 of the DSU says

> Panels may seek information from any relevant source and may consult experts to obtain their opinion on certain aspects of the matter. With respect to a factual issue concerning a scientific or other technical matter raised by a party to a dispute, a panel may request an advisory report in writing from an expert review group. Rules for the establishment of such a group and its procedures are set forth in Appendix 4.

Appendix 4 of the DSU contains more detailed provisions concerning the selection of independent experts, the right of the Panel to set terms of reference for the expert group and the process by which the expert group's opinions are made available to the Parties before the Panel decides on the use of the expert advice.

The Appellate Body has endorsed panel practice, so far, giving panels wide latitude in their use of expert advice. It has also endorsed the use of individual experts, rather than an expert group, where the panel deems it appropriate. Given this latitude, it appears that Panels may decide to consider any information from any person in addition to the Parties to the dispute – although they are under no obligation to do so and normally have no procedures for doing so.

The Appeal Process

The Appeals process is the most visible institutional innovation in the WTO dispute settlement system. No such institution existed in the GATT system and none exists in any other international legal context.

The function of the Appellate Body is to hear appeals on issues of law covered in a panel report and legal interpretations developed by a panel (Articles 17.1 and 17.6 of the DSU). The focus on issues of law and legal interpretation means that the Appellate Body does not review the panel's assessment of the facts of a case unless a claim is made that a panel failed to make an 'objective assessment of the facts' under Article 11 of the DSU.

The Appellate Body is a standing body – unlike the Panels that are established only for a particular case. It comprises seven persons who serve three at a time to hear any appeal. Its members are appointed by the DSB for four-year terms although a member may be reappointed once. The current membership of the Appellate Body includes prominent academics, judges and trade officials with extensive expertise in law, trade policy and economics. Although appointment to the Appellate Body is merit-based, the DSU recognizes the need for Appellate Body members to represent the diversity of Members' legal systems and traditions.

(i) The need for appellate process

The Appellate Body protects the interests of Members by ensuring that the 'automatic' dispute settlement system does not produce unsound decisions that could upset the balance of rights and obligations under the Agreements or affect the reasoning of future panels or the expectations of Members implementing the Agreements.

(ii) What does the Appellate Body review?

An appeal is limited by the provisions of Article 17.6 of the DSU to issues of law arising in the panel report and legal interpretations developed by the panel. However, 'issues of law' include not only the panel's legal interpretations of WTO provisions, but also the conduct of its processes under the procedural requirements of the DSU. The Appellate Body will, for example, review claims that the panel failed to make an objective assessment of the facts under Article 11 of the DSU or failed to accord due process to a party.

(iii) Basis of legal interpretations

Article 11 of the DSU requires the Panel to make 'an objective assessment of the matter before it, including an objective assessment of the facts of the case and the applicability of and conformity with the relevant covered agreements'. Where this means clarifying the meaning of the Agreements as they apply to the facts of the case, the Appellate Body has declared on numerous occasions that the legal interpretations of panels must be based on:

The 'general rule of interpretation' established by Article 31 of the Vienna Convention on the Law of Treaties, according to which the provisions of the WTO agreement must be interpreted 'in good faith in accordance with the ordinary meaning to be given to the terms of the treaty in their context and in the light of its object and purpose'. The Appellate Body has further elaborated the 'general rule' of interpretation by adding, 'interpretation must give meaning and effect to all the terms of the treaty. An interpreter is not free to adopt a reading that would result in reducing whole clauses or paragraphs of a treaty to redundancy or inutility' (see United States – Reformulated Gasoline WT/DS2/AB/R, p. 23).

A supplementary rule of interpretation in Article 32 of the Vienna Convention (see case Japan – Alcoholic beverages, WT/DS8/AB/R) that takes account of 'the preparatory work of the treaty and the circumstances of its conclusion' when the text of the treaty is ambiguous or obscure or leads to a result that is 'manifestly absurd or unreasonable'.

Article 3:2 of the DSU, according to which the WTO dispute settlement process 'serves to preserve the rights and obligations of Members under the covered agreement' and 'cannot add to or diminish the rights and obligations' of Members.

Article XVI:1 of the Agreement Establishing the WTO, according to which 'the WTO shall be guided by the decisions, procedures and customary practices followed by the CONTRACTING PARTIES to GATT 1947.'

(iv) Review of 'objective assessment'

When it has been asked to decide whether the Panel had fulfilled its obligation to make an 'objective assessment' of the facts, the Appellate Body has construed this obligation in such a way that an appeal on this ground will be very difficult to sustain.

In the case EC – Poultry Products (WT/DS69/AB/R, p.133), the Appellate Body said that an allegation that the panel failed to comply with its duty to make an objective assessment 'is a very serious allegation' which, 'goes to the very core of the integrity of the WTO dispute settlement process itself'. In EC – Hormones (WT/DS26/AB/R also at 133), the Appellate Body said an appeal would not be upheld because the Panel made a simple error of judgment in the appreciation of the evidence but only if the Panel made 'an egregious error that calls into question the good faith of the panel'. For such a claim to succeed, there must be evidence of a deliberate disregard, willful distortion or misrepresentation of the evidence on the part of panel.

(v) Review of Panel request

The Appellate Body has apparently tried not to complicate Members' resort to the dispute settlement system and has insisted that any dispute must be approached 'in good faith' by all sides.

For example, the Appellate Body has indicated that failure by a complainant to strictly comply with the procedural rules of the DSU – for example in making a request for a panel – does not automatically void the panel process. The Appellate Body has emphasized that Article 3.10 of the DSU commits Members in a dispute to engage in dispute settlement procedures 'in good faith in an effort to resolve the dispute'. This requires that both complaining and responding Members comply with the requirements of the DSU in good faith. In the case United States – Tax Treatment of Foreign Sales Corporations (FSC) (WT/DS108/ AB/R at 166) the Appellate Body clarified what this 'good faith' means:

> By good faith compliance, complaining Members accord to the responding Members the full measure of protection and opportunity to defend, contemplated by the letter and spirit of the procedural rules. The same principle of good faith requires that responding Members seasonably and promptly bring claimed procedural deficiencies to the attention of the complaining Member, and to the DSB or the Panel, so that corrections, if needed, can be made to resolve disputes. The procedural rules of WTO dispute settlement are designed to promote, not the development of litigation techniques, but simply the fair, prompt and effective resolution of trade disputes.

(vi) What can the Appellate Body do?

The Appellate Body is a standing body without 'terms of reference' such as those provided to a Panel on a case-by-case basis. Under Article 17.13 of the DSU, the Appellate Body has powers to uphold, modify or reverse the legal findings and conclusions of the panel. The only additional stipulation is that the Appellate Body 'shall address each of the issues' raised in the Parties' appeal(s).

The recommendations that the Appellate Body forwards to the DSB – along with the recommendations of the Panel – reflect the changes, if any that it has made to the Panel report. The Parties to the dispute must accept the decisions of the Appellate Body 'unconditionally': which means that there is no further appeal from a decision of the Appellate Body.

Where the Appellate Body has reversed a panel's legal conclusion on a measure, it has decided on some occasions to 'complete the legal analysis' by making a finding on a legal issue which was not addressed by the panel. For example, in Canada – Certain Measures Concerning Periodicals, the Appellate Body reversed the panel's findings on the issue of 'like products' under the first sentence of Article III:2 of the GATT 1994 and proceeded to examine the consistency of the measure with the second sentence of Article III:2

(WT/DS31/AB/R pp. 23 and 24). Similarly, the Appellate Body in *United States – Shrimp* considered its responsibility to complete the analysis and secure a positive solution to a dispute as provided by Article 3.7 of the DSU, where 'the facts on the record of the panel proceedings permit' (WT/DS58/AB/R p. 124).

(vii) What processes does the Appellate Body follow?

The Working Procedures for Appellate Review (WT/AB/WP/3) contain detailed provisions on duties, responsibilities and rules of conduct of Appellate Body members, the process of appellate review, and timetables. The timetable for the Appellate Body is tight, considering that the seven members may be reviewing several cases at the same time. Article 17 of the DSU requires that, as a general rule, proceedings should not exceed 60 days from the date a party formally notifies its decision to appeal to the date the Appellate Body circulates its report (and must not, in any case, exceed 90 days).

Between the circulation of the final version of the Panel report and the DSB meeting at which the Panel's recommendations will be considered, parties to the dispute may appeal the Panel recommendations by notifying the DSB and the WTO Secretariat. Within ten days of the notice, the appellant must lodge a detailed statement of appeal including:

- A precise statement of the grounds for the appeal, including the specific allegations of errors in the issues of law covered in the panel report and legal interpretations developed by the panel, and the legal arguments in support thereof;
- A precise statement of the provisions of the covered agreements and other legal sources relied on; and
- The nature of the decision or ruling sought.

Any other party to the dispute may, within 25 days of the notice of appeal, lodge a written submission, with similar content, rebutting the allegations in the appeal. Only parties to the dispute may appeal a panel report. However, Article 17.4 of the DSU stipulates that third parties who have notified the DSB of a substantial interest in the matter may make written submissions and be provided an opportunity to be heard by the Appellate Body.

Given the short timetable, the Appellate Body must quickly establish a timetable for written submissions and an 'oral' hearing (within five days of receiving the submission from parties opposed to the appeal). In effect the 'oral' hearing procedures are themselves mostly written procedures.

(viii) Who may appear before the Appellate Body?

As in the case of Panels, only the delegates of Member governments may participate in a meeting with the Appellate Body. The 'oral' hearing is not an open meeting. As in the case of Panels it is a matter for the Member involved to determine the composition of their delegation.

Table 6: Timetable for appeals

	General Appeals (Day)	Prohibited Subsidies Appeals (Day)
Notice of Appeal	0	0
Appellant's Submission	10	5
Other Appellant(s) Submission(s)	15	7
Appellee(s) Submission(s)	25	12
Third Participant(s) Submission(s)	25	12
Oral Hearing	30	15
Circulation of Appellate Report	60–90	30–60
DSB Meeting for Adoption	90–120	50–80

The Appellate Body decided on a request by St Lucia in the EC – Bananas Case (WT/DS27/AB/R, pp. 10–12) that there was nothing in WTO or GATT provision or practice that determined who could represent a Member in a Panel meeting with parties or who could represent a Member at the oral hearings of the Appellate Body. It therefore raised no objections to St Lucia appointing two lawyers who were not government officials to represent it in the oral hearing. Furthermore, the Appellate Body endorsed the practice: 'given the Appellate Body's mandate to review only issues of law or legal interpretation in panel reports, it is particularly important that governments be represented by qualified counsel in Appellate Body proceedings' (WT/DS27/AB/R, p. 12).

Although Panels may decide for themselves whom to consult other than the parties to a dispute, the Appellate Body has generally deferred to the Members, allowing parties to exercise their discretion not only about representation at hearings but also about the inclusion of submissions from non-government organizations. In the US – Shrimp case, the Appellate Body allowed the United States to attach three submissions from non-government organizations to its own submission. The Appellate Body said that it would consider these to form part of the US submission *and* would consider them in its deliberations to the extent that he views that they expressed were adopted by the US as its own views. As it turned out, the US provided only qualified endorsement of the additional submissions and the Appellate Body, while accepting them as part of the US submission, did not consider them further.

In a notice of procedural decision (WT/DS135/9) related to hearings in a later case – EU – Asbestos – the Appellate Body appeared, for once, to depart from this deferential posture. In response to a large number of requests, it established, on its own authority, a set of procedures for non-government bodies to submit so-called *amicus-curiae* ('friends of court') briefs for possible consideration – at the Appellate Body's discretion. This procedural initiative was, however, strongly criticized by Members in the DSB, – many of whom – particularly developing countries – are opposed to any further opening of the dispute settlement system to non-government organizations, whether as *amicus-curiae* or observers or in any other capacity.

(ix) Consequences of 'judicial' processes

Is the Appellate Body a 'judicial' body? The creation of the Appellate Body certainly gives the dispute settlement system a *more judicial* character than it had under the GATT. The judicial character of its work is emphasized by:

- The 'collegiality' of the Appellate Body, which allocates joint responsibility to each 'division' for its decisions
- The continuing mandate of the Appellate Body – in contrast to the temporary mandate of the Panels
- The finality of its decisions on matters of law: there's no further appeal from the Appellate Body.

It appears that the drafters of the DSU intended this new judicial orientation in the dispute settlement system to establish more certainty and predictability in the interpretation of the Agreements as they apply to particular disputes.

There had been a slow but progressive movement, even under the GATT, towards more certain and predictable processes based on better legal understanding of the Agreements. At first, under GATT there were no 'panels' only *ad hoc* working groups established to deal with disputes. Then in the 1950s the Panel system was introduced to provide more focused, written advice to the GATT Council. Panels – although comprising mostly diplomats from GATT missions – dealt with progressively more difficult issues as GATT turned its attention to non-tariff barriers in the 1970s: issues where the text of the GATT itself was often ambiguous and even deficient. Eventually, in the 1980s, the need for careful, sophisticated reasoning about the nature of the obligations in the GATT and in the Tokyo Round non-tariff barrier 'codes' prompted the creation of a small legal unit in the GATT secretariat to assist with disputes.

There are obvious benefits that flow from the certainty and precision that legal reasoning and procedures bring to the WTO dispute settlement system; especially the protection they offer for Members' rights under the 'automatic' decision-making procedures. But there are also some potential costs. Some commentators suggest that the creation of a 'court like' institution inside the WTO could change the character of the Organization or affect its ability to settle disputes. Academic analysts, civil society groups and even Member government officials are asking questions such as:

- Is there a danger that a 'court-like' institution could supplant the authority of Members by making 'new' rules through appellate decisions that are difficult (if not impossible) to overturn in the DSB, given the requirement for a negative consensus to do so?
- Is there a danger that a 'court-like' institution could encourage an harmful climate of 'legalism' in the WTO, where the resolution of differences by negotiation, compromise and mutual agreement among sovereigns would be replaced by litigious procedures managed by – and for the profit of – law firms?

There has been too little experience of the WTO dispute settlement system, so far, to answer these speculative questions. Many commentators and practitioners argue that the system needs time to adjust to dramatic changes such as binding arbitration and appeals. It does appear, however, that the high volume of cases brought since 1995 is testing the system thoroughly, so more definitive answers to these questions may appear in the near future simply as a matter of practice. Or, maybe the questions will change.

For the present, a robust debate continues outside – and even inside – the WTO on the role of the new institutions and over the new 'legal' processes. Here's how some of the arguments and counter-arguments line up ('no punches pulled'!):

Could the Appellate Body 'make new rules'?

Yes: and it's doing that already	No: they don't and they can't
It looks like the Appellate Body decided to rule on issues that were not the subject of appeal in order to 'resolve a dispute' in the Shrimp-Turtle case. In that case it re-interpreted part of the GATT 1994 Agreement (Article XX) by constructing an interpretation from an Agreement not mentioned in the complaint (the Marrakesh Agreement Establishing WTO).	The Appellate Body was urged to 'complete the analysis' of Article XX by some appellants in the case because the Panel report erred in its interpretation. It is, after all, part of the Appellate Body's duty to help find a solution to the dispute and it did this by showing that the measures did not comply with one part of Article XX.
The Appellate Body seems prepared to add and subtract rights by 'interpreting' the Agreements and even the 'negotiators' intentions'! Consider the 'creative' interpretation that it gave to the meaning of GATT Article XX in Shrimp-Turtle, and the continuing force it gave to old GATT 'safeguard' language in the Argentina – Footwear case (WT/DS121).	Not true! First, the Appellate Body has adopted standard legal interpretation procedures that rely on the plain meaning of the text of the agreements taken in context – including the negotiating context. This is what the Vienna Convention requires. Second, it repeatedly defers to the DSU stipulation that nothing it does can add to or subtract from Members' rights.
The Appellate Body decision to accept 'amicus curiae' submissions from Non-Government Organizations in the EC-Asbestos case seems to show that they are prepared to establish their own procedures without reference to the Members – and even to accept direct lobbying by non-members such as the NGOs.	Many Members were clearly unhappy about this decision. But it was only a procedural matter, within the competence of the Appellate Body and related to one case only – in which the Appellate Body rightly anticipated a great deal of public interest. The Appellate Body has already shown, in Shrimp-Turtle, however, that it is very conscious of its duty to distinguish those submissions that represent Members' views and those that do not. They made it very clear that they were under no obligation to consider any views from 'amicus' submissions.
Even if the Appellate Body does not seek to impose its interpretations on the Agreements, won't it be pressured by disputants to 'fill in' the gaps and ambiguities in the Agreements, left when the negotiators failed to reach agreement on details?	If there is ambiguity in an Agreement then the Appellate Body may indeed be required to interpret the Agreement using approaches provided in the Vienna Convention (including Article 32). But the recommendation if adopted will bind only the parties to the particular dispute. Ambiguities are no longer a 'cost free' solution for negotiators who can't agree. But this is hardly the fault of the Appellate Body and could turn out to be a positive discipline.

Could the new 'legalism' replace negotiated agreements with litigation?

Yes, and its already happening	No, there are safeguards in place
The WTO Agreements have already started to replace the 'outcomes' based disciplines of GATT with detailed implementation rules such as those in the TRIPS Agreement that embody specific standards all Members must adopt. Aren't Members loosing control over their own trade policies?	This concern is exaggerated. Most Agreements are still 'outcomes'-based: they contain no policy formulas and allow Members wide latitude of choice in the implementation of WTO principles and rules. The Appellate Body has, in fact, acted to preserve the widest possible discretion for Members in some of its highest-profile decisions. For example in US – Reformulated Gasoline it acknowledged that WTO members have broad autonomy to determine their own policies on the environment. It rolled back the Panel's narrow interpretations of SPS obligations in EC – Hormones and went a long way to defer to Member state policies – against the Panel's reasoning – in US – Shrimp-turtle Some expert commentators (e.g. Prof John Jackson) argue that the Appellate Body has shown much greater deference to Members' policy autonomy than the GATT Panels did.
Isn't the greatly increased caseload in the dispute settlement system evidence that lawyers are loose in the WTO and looking to build up business?	The case load has increased by comparison with GATT, but so has membership and the level of membership *participation*. The increased caseload may be due to the greater confidence Members have in the new, more 'automatic' procedures or to the much larger membership of WTO or to the universal coverage of the Agreements. In fact, only one third of notified WTO disputes are proceeding to a Panel recommendation. There is no evidence that 'litigious' behavior is driving the number of cases.
Are the major economies using the dispute settlement system as a 'weapon' to gain leverage in unrelated disputes? Hasn't there been evidence of 'tit-for-tat' disputes between the major economies?	The Appellate Body made it very clear in US – FSC (WT/DS108/AB/R at 166) that the WTO dispute settlement system has no room for litigation techniques, but only for the fair, prompt and effective resolution of disputes It has repeatedly emphasized the requirement of the DSU that all Members approach the resolution of disputes in good faith and has refused appeals where it found 'good faith' lacking.
Isn't there a danger with the new 'legal' processes that some Members will try to litigate issues that they could not negotiate in the WTO – for example by seeking rulings that 'fill-in' ambiguities in the Agreements.	It's hard to think of any examples of this. Cases brought so far that have tested the 'edges' of the Agreements – such as Shrimp-Turtle or Japan – Photographic Paper – have not been successful for the parties seeking to 'extend' ambiguous aspects of the Agreements. The Appellate Body may be required to rule on ambiguous articles, but it has already established a standard procedure for doing so that has long been used for the interpretation of other treaties. Besides, recommendations by the Panels and the Appellate body, if adopted by the DSB, do not bind any Member other than the Parties in a particular case.

The Dispute Settlement Body

What's left for the Council of Members – the DSB – to do, in the new 'automatic' dispute settlement system? They seem to have lost their discretion to establish a Panel or to accept Panel or Appellate Body recommendations. Has the dispute settlement system left the DSB as a 'figurehead'? Members retain, in fact, all of the key powers to decide but a less active role in the process. One way of looking at the system is that the DSB has 'legislative' powers that may be used to override the 'judicial' powers of the Panels and the Appellate Body – but are unlikely to be used in this way in the normal course of events.

The DSB has the power to

- Appoint Panelists and adopt terms of reference for Panels
- Adopt or reject a recommendation of a Panel or the Appellate Body – at least in principle
- Maintain surveillance of the implementation of recommendations
- Appoint arbitrators to make recommendations on the 'reasonable period of time'
- Appoint a second, 'implementation' Panel to make recommendations on measures to restore conformity with the Agreement(s)
- Authorize the suspension of concessions or obligations (retaliation).

Appointment of panelists and panel terms of reference: since each Panel is 'ad-hoc', the power to appoint is significant, with important potential consequences for the decision on the case. The DSU gives disputants some say in the appointments, but the ultimate decision rests with the DSB. The power to adopt terms of reference for a Panel is less significant. The terms of reference themselves are very important: they put a perimeter around the matters into which the Panel may enquire. The Appellate Body has repeatedly emphasized their importance, too, in ensuring a fair hearing for the complainant and a fair opportunity for the respondent to prepare its case. The parties may agree terms of reference that the DSB may approve, but the DSU provides standard terms if no agreement is forthcoming so that the DSB discretion in this matter is limited.

Adoption of panel and Appellate Body reports: Panel recommendations have no binding force and do not give rise to obligations on the defending party to bring its measures into conformity *unless* they are adopted by the DSB. Under the GATT dispute settlement system, panel reports were adopted by consensus, i.e. where no delegation present at the meeting objected to the adoption of a report. This gave respondent parties the opportunity to block adverse reports simply by refusing to join a consensus. It was not a common occurrence – but the opportunity itself was sufficient to make it a fundamental weakness of the GATT dispute settlement system.

A panel report must be adopted at a DSB meeting within 60 days after the date of circulation to the Members, unless a party to the dispute notifies its decision to appeal or if the DSB decides by consensus not to adopt the report

(Article 16.4 of the DSU). An Appellate Body report must be adopted by the DSB and unconditionally accepted by the parties to the dispute within 30 days after its circulation, unless the DSB decides by consensus not to adopt the report (DSU Article 17.14).

'Consensus against' – an impossible hurdle?

The procedure by which the DSB adopts a Panel report is remarkable for two reasons. First, it is the only part of the WTO where a decision (to adopt) is 'automatic' in the absence of a negative consensus. Second, the consensus procedure in the DSB has no 'fall-back' voting formula. In other WTO provisions where consensus is the 'preferred' decision-making process, there are detailed provisions for 'fall-back' qualified majority voting: for example in Article X of the Agreement Establishing the WTO. The standard in the DSB is set higher: consensus or nothing.

But the achievement of 'consensus' – even negative consensus – is not quite the hurdle that it appears to be. The 'consensus rule' appears to be a great 'leveler', removing all distinctions between Members based on power or interest because every Member, individually, has an equal ability to upset a consensus. In practice, however, the procedure is more nuanced since in a consensus decision Members are not asked to declare their views unless they oppose the proposition. Neither absence nor abstention counts against a consensus. So Members may defer to the greater interest of those directly affected by a decision or to the wishes of more powerful economies, allowing the consensus to proceed by silently abstaining *without thereby agreeing* with the proposition. It is very likely that many consensus decisions in the WTO succeed on the basis of widespread 'abstention' rather than on the basis of a true consensus of opinion.

'Consensus against' may not be an *impossible* hurdle for the DSB to vault, after all.

Surveillance of implementation: There is no power in the DSU to require *specific action* by a Member to implement a DSB recommendation or ruling: Members of the WTO always retain the right to shape their own policies and regulations as long as they conform with its obligations under the Agreements. The one exception in the DSU concerns rulings under Article 4.7 of the Agreement on Subsidies and Countervailing Measures. In this case, where a measure is found to be a prohibited subsidy, the panel 'shall recommend that the subsidizing Member withdraw the subsidy without delay'.

The normal format of DSB decisions on a dispute is to approve the recommendations of the Panels – as amended by the Appellate Body – that a member restore conformity of its measures with the Agreement(s). The responding party is expected to make the appropriate changes, possibly in line with suggestions

'Reasonable period of time'

Ultimately this period of time for implementation may be determined by the DSB according to the circumstances of a case, but the DSU emphasizes that 'prompt' compliance action is 'essential' (Articles 3.3. and 21.1). The Understanding recommends no longer than 15 months from the date of adoption of the Panel report and Arbitrators have tended to treat this as the maximum period.

There have been some attempts by Arbitrators to establish 'jurisprudence' on the 'reasonable period of time'. In the *Canada – Patent Protection of Pharmaceuticals* case, the Arbitrator suggested that a reasonable period would be longer where legislative amendments were required than if administrative action, such as changes to regulations, would effect implementation (WT/DS114/13 at 49).

In this and other cases, Arbitrators have ruled that the management of the consequences of the required action are not relevant considerations in determining the 'reasonable' period. The reasonable period of time would not, for example, include time for 'structural adjustment' of an affected domestic industry (*ibid.* at 52). Claims that the summer vacation period should be taken into account in calculating the reasonable period of time have also been rejected (*ibid.* at 61).

---

from the Panel – although so far these have been offered in only one or two cases. In many cases the respondent party informs the DSB at the meeting where the report of the Panel is adopted that it intends to take steps to implement the recommendations within a period of time that has been agreed in advance with the complainant, or is a period of time acceptable to the DSB. The DSB, after adopting the Panel report, maintains an item on its regular agenda under which it receives reports from the complainant and/or respondent on the status of implementation. The item is removed once both parties signal that the implementation is complete.

Appoint arbitrators or a second Panel: Implementation does not always go so smoothly. There are four outcomes contemplated in the DSU that imply a decision by the DSB:

1. The respondent makes a proposal for implementation that is acceptable to the complainant and completes implementation within a 'reasonable period of time' that may be agreed between the parties or is acceptable to the DSB. This is the 'normal' case.
2. There is a 'disagreement as to the existence or consistency' of the implementing measures and the DSB establishes an 'implementation Panel' (preferably the same Panel as made the initial recommendations on the case),

under Article 21.5 of the DSU, to make recommendations within 90 days on implementation.
3. In either case (1) or (2), if the parties are unable to agree on a 'reasonable period of time' for the restoration of conformity with the Agreement(s) and the respondent does not propose a period for implementation that is acceptable to the DSB, the DSB appoints an arbitrator to recommend a period.
4. The respondent fails to make any proposal for implementation or fails to implement the recommendations of the second Panel within a reasonable period of time, in which case it may offer compensation – as a temporary measure – or the complainant may request authorization from the DSB for the suspension of obligations or concessions (retaliation).

Implementing dispute decisions

Implementation can be straightforward when the parties to a dispute agree on the manner and timing. Many cases that are pursued to the final Panel report do end in agreement between the Parties and nothing more is heard of the problem. Problems arise, however, when the Parties do not agree on implementation and experience has shown that the DSU does not necessarily have the answers to these problems.

Problems specifying 'rectification': 'Rectification' means 'putting things right'. That's what the outcome of any dispute should be. Contrary to widespread belief the WTO doesn't, in general, try to tell Members – who are sovereign governments – what they must do to comply with their obligations under the Agreements. So the dispute settlement process ends only with a direction to the 'losing' Member to bring its measures into conformity with the Agreements *somehow or other*. If the 'somehow or other' is not proposed by the respondent or is not satisfactory to the complainant or the DSB, the DSB may re-activate the disputes procedure with a second Panel established to develop a recommendation on implementing measures.

But several matters about this process are unclear: for example, under Article 21.5, the DSU says nothing about the terms of reference for this Panel or about the opportunity for the Parties to object to its decisions or appeal them if they are legally unsound. There is also another problem with this Article – its relationship to the 'retaliation' procedures in Article 22 (see below).

Problems with enforcement: The WTO does not have any enforcement mechanisms of its own: it has no economic powers, it doesn't issue fines and it can't tell sovereign members what precise policy decisions they must make. Enforcement, if needed, takes the form of authorized actions between the parties.

If the respondent does not implement a decision or implementation is unreasonably delayed, the DSB may authorize temporary, and voluntary, compensation for an inconsistent measure – to be offered by the respondent pending restoration of compliance. Or, as a last resort, the DSB may authorize the complainant to withdraw concessions (e.g. increase tariffs) or suspend its obligations to the respondent under the Agreements. But the procedure for deciding on appropriate compensation or retaliation – potentially involving still further arbitration on the level of compensation – is very complex and not well defined in the DSU (Article 22) and is the focus of some continuing controversy among Members.

(i) Compensation

Article 22 of the DSU says that where a Member fails to implement the recommendations and rulings of the DSB within the 'reasonable period of time' the DSB may authorize compensation or the suspension of concessions (retaliation).

Compensation is a sort of temporary 'band-aid' relief for damage caused by a violation of WTO rules. The DSU is very specific in saying that it is not intended to be a substitute for bringing measures into conformity with the Agreements (Article 22.1). You can see why: if it were to be permitted as a permanent solution to a dispute then large Member economies – especially – might use compensation to 'buy their way out' of their obligation to conform with the Agreements.

'Compensation' is *not* financial compensation. It usually takes the form of improved access to the responding Member's market, is voluntary, and if granted must be consistent with the WTO Agreements (Article 22.2). For example, compensation in the form of tariff reductions must be applied on a Most-Favoured-Nation (MFN) basis, i.e. it must be extended to the like products of all WTO Members, not just that of the complainant. If compensation is not agreed within 20 days after the expiry of the reasonable period of time, the complainant may request the DSB to authorize the suspension of concessions (retaliation).

(ii) Retaliation

'Retaliation' takes the form of the suspension of equivalent concessions or obligations that would normally be owed by the complainant party to the respondent party. It is usually in the form of punitive tariffs (100% *ad valorem*) on selected product items from the respondent country, applied over and above the normal tariff rate in the complainant country. This measure represents a suspension of the complainant's obligations to bind its tariff rates and to offer the respondent MFN tariff treatment. A 'retaliatory' tariff is likely to eliminate the responding Member's exports of the particular product.

Article 22.4 of the DSU requires that the suspended concessions be equivalent to the level of nullification or impairment suffered as a result of the measure found to be WTO-inconsistent. In the event of disagreement between the parties on the level of proposed retaliation, Articles 22.6 and 22.7 of the DSU provide for arbitration. Arbitration in the EC – Bananas and EC – Hormones cases has shown that complainants may greatly overstate the impact of the nullification and impairment: the awards in these cases have been much lower than the original requests.

WTO Members have disagreed about the sequence of events that precedes a complainant's rights to request retaliation. Unfortunately, it turns out that there is an ambiguity in the text of the DSU:

- Article 21.5 of the DSU calls for the original panel to decide any disagreement about implementing measures within 90 days of the 'date of referral of the matter to it', *and*
- Article 22.6 of the DSU calls for an arbitrated award of 'retaliation' within 60 days of the expiry of the 'reasonable period of time'.

The DSU does not say whether complaining Members may request the authorization of retaliation *before* the completion of Article 21.5 processes examining the consistency of implementing measures, or whether Article 21.5 panel decisions may be appealed, or whether the complainant has the right to an arbitral award of retaliation under Article 22.6 pending any appeal outcome. The controversy reflects the concern of respondent parties that that complaining Members could take matters into their own hands *and* the concern of complainants that respondents might use the second panel process under Article 21.5 – possibly over and over again – to delay implementation.

Fortunately, so far, most Parties have agreed between them on procedures to work around this ambiguity. In *Brazil – Aircraft Subsidies*, Brazil and Canada agreed that:

- Brazil would not object to the establishment of an Article 21.5 panel;
- Canada would not request authorization to suspend concessions until after circulation of the Article 21.5 report;
- In the event of a finding of non-conformity by the Article 21.5 panel, Canada would request authorization for suspension and Brazil could request arbitration under Article 22.6 of the DSU (WT/DS46/13 Annex).

A 'sequencing' problem

'This [sequencing] issue is vividly illustrated in the *Bananas* dispute opposing the EC and the United States. The Appellate Body report condemned the EC bananas policy and requested the EC to bring their measures into compliance with their obligations. As a result, the EC made some changes to its policy, but the United States alleged that the implementing actions were inadequate and that the policy was still at odds with the EC's obligations under the WTO. Since there was disagreement between the parties to the dispute as to the adequacy of the implementing action, a [Article 21.5] panel was established to decide the issue. At

---

A 'sequencing' problem *cont'd*

this stage, the parties could no longer agree on the interpretation of the DSU. According to the EC, a finding by a panel that the implementing action is inadequate must precede a request to adopt countermeasures. The United States however … requested the panel to also rule on whether the proposed countermeasures by the US were equivalent with the damage the US suffered from the EC bananas policy. Furthermore, the United States imposed countermeasures (to be repaid if the US lost the case, as the US have claimed) even before the panel had pronounced on the equivalence of the US proposed countermeasures.'

Horn, H. and Mavroidis, P. C. *'Remedies In The WTO Dispute Settlement System And Developing Country Interests'*, World Bank 1999, p. 17.

A similar agreement was reached in Brazil's complaint in *Canada – Aircraft Subsidies*. Following the finding by the Article 21.5 ('implementation') panel in *Brazil – Aircraft Subsidies* that Brazil's measures were still WTO-inconsistent, Brazil notified its intention to appeal at the 22 May 2000 DSB meeting and requested arbitration on the level of nullification or impairment (under Article 22.6). Canada also stated it would not seek to apply suspension pending the Appellate Body and arbitration reports on the implementation Panel report. The Appellate Body rejected Brazil's appeals in both *Brazil – Aircraft Subsidies* and *Canada – Aircraft Subsidies*.

But some of the disagreements on the 'sequencing' issue have been the cause of large-scale trade frictions (see text box 'A sequencing problem') and have, in the view of some commentators, prompted additional, litigious action in the WTO.

Cross-sector retaliation: One of the important innovations of the DSU as compared with the former GATT dispute settlement system was the provision in Article 22.3 for suspensions of obligations and concessions:

- Under Agreements other than the Agreement breached by the respondent, or
- In sectors (goods, services, intellectual property) other than the sector of trade in which the breach took place.

This 'cross-sector retaliation' was a hard-fought issue between some developed and developing countries during the Uruguay Round of trade negotiations; developing countries expressing concern that measures taken against their goods trade in retaliation for deficiencies in their compliance with rules in the 'new' sectors of WTO activities would jeopardize their development plans.

As it turned out, the first significant use of the provision was by a developing country: Ecuador, in the *EC – Bananas* case.

On 8 November 1999, Ecuador requested authorization from the DSB to suspend the application to the European Communities of concessions or other obligations under the TRIPS Agreement, GATS and GATT 1994, in an amount of US$450 million. At the request of the European Communities, the DSB referred the issue of the level of suspension to the original panel for arbitration. The decision of the arbitrators was circulated to WTO Members on 24 March 2000. The arbitrators found that the level of nullification or impairment suffered by Ecuador amounted to US$201.6 million per year. The arbitrators found that Ecuador may request authorization by the DSB to suspend concessions or other obligations under the GATT 1994 (not including investment goods or primary goods used as inputs in manufacturing and processing industries); under the GATS with respect to 'wholesale trade services' (CPC 622) in the principal distribution services; and, to the extent that suspension requested under GATT 1994 and GATS was insufficient to reach the level of nullification and impairment determined by the arbitrators, under TRIPS in a number of sectors of that Agreement. After Ecuador had modified its request in conformity with the arbitrator's findings, the DSB authorized Ecuador, on 18 May 2000, to suspend concessions to the European Communities equivalent to US$201.6 million.

WTO Annual Report, 2000

Retaliation is an 'asymmetric' discipline and tends to backfire: The withdrawal of equivalent obligations or concessions is less likely to be an effective threat when the complainant is a small economy. A small economy is unlikely to have the 'weight' to inflict much pain on a larger economy, which probably has a wide range of alternative market opportunities. Not even the use of cross-sector retaliation or un-sanctioned 'carousel' methods of retaliation is likely to improve the 'leverage' of a small economy. Furthermore, the increase in protection for one or two specific sectors in the complainant country, particularly a small complainant country, is very likely to be harmful for its own economy: raising the domestic price of inputs or final goods, reducing consumption, distorting investment in the long term by adding artificially to the returns to specialized factors of production. The more significant the traded items that are caught up in the retaliatory action, the more noxious the action will be for the complainant's economy. The 'carousel' method may reduce the structural damage – assuming it does not have the same domestic impact on investment or wages etc in the protected sectors.

Retaliation is rare: (fortunately!) Why? We can speculate that there are two reasons. First, most countries are aware of its limited value (see previous paragraph). Second, trade and economic relations in the WTO – or foreign relations generally – are a 'repeated game', to use strategic terms. This means that there is likely to be a positive 'payoff' in the next 'round' of engagements if you cooperate now. There is also likely to be an adverse payoff in the next 'round' for 'defection' or 'non-cooperation' now. It's a lot like the 'golden rule': what you do to your trading partners today, maybe done to you tomorrow. The WTO principle of 'reciprocity' in trade negotiations makes this simple strategic consideration explicit. So, most countries cooperate most of the time: whether or not they agree with the decision, they accept the DSB's ruling with as much good grace as they can, withdraw or amend the offending measure and *move on.*

Role of the Secretariat

The Secretariat plays a very important role in the dispute settlement system: providing impartial assistance to the Chairman of the DSB, to the Panels and to the Appellate Body. The Secretariat also provides limited legal assistance to developing countries and technical assistance, in the form of training courses, under Article 27 of the DSU.

In practice, the role of the Secretariat is a delicate one. Article 27 gives some clues:

> The Secretariat shall have the responsibility of assisting panels, especially on the legal, historical and procedural aspects of the matters dealt with, and of providing secretarial and technical support.

Because the Panels are 'ad-hoc' and the Appellate Body has a limited remit to *review* cases, the Secretariat frequently finds itself called upon to provide the institutional memory and the experience that Panels need when deciding how to go about their work. The Secretariat provides, in fact, some of the 'continuity' that creates a 'system' out of a series of WTO dispute cases (of course the DSB and the Appellate Body also contribute to this continuity). This is what the DSU means by 'assisting panels … [with] the legal, historical and procedural aspects of the matters dealt with …' In fact, the Chairman of the DSB frequently calls on the experience and 'continuity' represented in the Secretariat when composing a list of Panelists to propose to disputants.

The 'secretarial and technical support' functions mentioned in Article 27 are also much more important than this modest reference suggests. The 'legal secretary' who is appointed by the Legal Division of the WTO Secretariat to work with each Panel can influence the Panel report by, for example, helping the members of the Panel with legal interpretations. The legal secretary can also assist the members of the Panel to manage the large documentary submissions that are becoming common in WTO cases by helping them to determine the key issues.

Developing country provisions

Most of the 'special and differential' treatment of developing-country interests in the WTO is found in the substantive agreements themselves where, almost without exception, there is provision for lower thresholds and longer timeframes for implementation of WTO obligations by developing countries.

The DSU also provides for longer time-frames for developing countries – including the possibility of extending the time for consultations and the time allowed by Panels for developing countries to prepare briefs (Article 12.10). Also, Panels are required to 'explicitly indicate' how they took account of relevant provisions on differential and more-favourable treatment for developing countries under the covered agreements if this matter is raised with them by developing-country parties (Article 12.11).

In ensuring implementation of decisions in cases bought by developing countries, the Understanding requires the DSB to take into account 'not only the trade coverage of measures complained of, but also their impact on the economy of developing-country Members concerned' (Article 21.8).

Article 24 of the DSU is devoted to the interests of least-developed countries – the poorest countries that are Members of the WTO. It urges Members to use 'due restraint' when considering whether to bring a formal complaint against a least-developed member and urges the use of the 'good offices' of the Director-General to try to ensure that matters are settled by consultation rather than proceed to a Panel request. If measures maintained by a least-developed member are found to nullify or impair benefits, to use restraint in considering whether to seek compensation or authorization for retaliation.

Chapter Three
Review of the DSU

Ministers… Invite the Ministerial Conference to complete a full review of dispute settlement rules and procedures under the World Trade Organization within four years after the entry into force of the Agreement Establishing the World Trade Organization, and to take a decision on the occasion of its first meeting after the completion of the review, whether to continue, modify or terminate such dispute settlement rules and procedures.

Decision on the application and review of the understanding on rules and procedures governing the settlement of disputes

Members at first expected to complete the review of the DSU by the end of 1998, in time for the Seattle Ministerial meeting. This would have allowed Ministers to make any required changes to the DSU. But the review was completed but no proposals were put to the Ministerial Council directly as a result of the Review. Several Members did submit a proposal for DSU amendments to the Third Session of the Ministerial Conference. However, a final agreement was not reached.

Subsequent to the Third Ministerial Conference several Members submitted a similar proposed amendment to the General Council for its consideration. As of July 2001, however, there was still no agreement on proposals to revise the DSU despite weeks of consultations and debate in the DSB. The focus of the proposal is the so-called 'sequencing' issue which can be described as follows:

'Sequencing': the relationship between Articles 21.5 and 22.6 of the DSU concerning the right of a 'winning' party to take retaliatory action under Art. 22.6 in the absence of compliance (in its view) by the 'loosing' party before recourse to procedures under Art. 21.5.

The proposal to amend the DSU would create a new Article 21 of the DSU that would clarify the sequencing issue related to Articles 21 and 22. The amended DSU would require a compliance panel to decide disagreements over measures taken to implement a panel or Appellate Body ruling before Members could request WTO authorization to impose retaliatory trade sanctions. The proposal also addressed some other issues such as time frames for disputes, third-party rights and certain aspects of special and differential treatment for developing countries. However, some Members remain dissatisfied with the proposal arguing that it does not go far enough on matters of transparency. Others did not consider it comprehensive enough.

A number of proposals on other matters have also been submitted to the DSB in the context of the review. Among these:

- The European Communities suggested that a body of 15–24 professional panelists be set up, from which panels could be created and have argued that greater weight should be given to consultations and to strengthen the rights of 'third parties' in a dispute.
- Developing countries argued that the DSU's special and differential treatment provisions in favor of developing countries have not yet given the benefits hoped for (although the creation of the Advisory Center on WTO Law is expected to meet some of those concerns).

Chapter Four
Should you bring a complaint?

Well, 'you' can bring a complaint to the WTO only if you're a Member government. But Governments usually bring cases that are prompted by some firm's commercial interests. So we'll imagine two cases:

- *First*, that you are an exporter or importer that has a problem with a foreign trade regulation.
- *Second*, that you are the advisor to the Trade Minister, trying to evaluate the options to put to the government.

In both cases the only way to decide whether 'you' should bring a complaint is to ask yourself what you want and then whether a WTO dispute procedure will get you what you want more effectively – lets say, at less 'cost' – than other means. So there are no surprises, we'll summarize the answers at the beginning:

If 'you' are a firm the two big problems you face are the time it takes to get regulations changed by the dispute settlement system and the limited value you can expect from the likely remedies if you win the case. Even if the government agrees quickly to do what you want and even if the problem is resolved at the 'consultation' stage, the chances are the timeframe could be too long for you. Markets, products and competitors will have moved on by the time the talks conclude. Even if your side 'wins', you may be no better off in a commercial sense because the main 'remedy' – restoration of conformity with the

Agreement(s) – could very well be just as 'bad' for you, commercially, as the initial problem and if it's 'good' then your competitors will probably benefit from the change, too. Finally, you can't deal with contract disputes in WTO: the International Chamber of Commerce (ICC) arbitration procedures are the way to cover that sort of problem.

If 'you' are a government, there are many circumstances where it might be worthwhile to notify a complaint and start the consultation process: but only after you'd tried other bilateral approaches. There are only a few circumstances where you'd want to pursue a complaint to a Panel recommendation and DSB decision: in fact, you'd probably do this only when there was really no other way to get what you want, because it's expensive and, potentially, risky.

In summary, when there's no other way, the WTO dispute settlement system offers an invaluable process for securing fair opportunities for trade in accordance with the provisions of the Agreements. But look at the alternatives carefully; they might offer better 'value' solutions in many cases.

You are a firm

You've identified a problem with your market that is due to the regulations or policies of a foreign government. It's not a matter covered in your contract with your customers or suppliers and it's not a risk you insured in your trade finance arrangements. You have some idea of what this problem is costing you (loss of sales, loss of growth opportunities) and what you would expect to gain (e.g. sales, lower costs) if the regulation were changed. What do you do?

(1) First exhaust your options for securing changes to the regulation by lobbying the foreign government. You might be able to do this on your own account: perhaps you have investments in the foreign market, or employees there. That may be sufficient to secure you an interview with the officials in the foreign government. Or you may be able to secure help from the foreign trade or diplomatic service of your own government to approach the officials of the foreign government seeking a change in the regulations. Perhaps your national Chamber of Commerce or industry Association might be able to help, too. Chances are, if your firm has a problem then others in your country or in your industry in other countries will have a similar problem – it may be possible to approach the foreign government through an industry group already working on the problem.

(2) Check with your own Trade Ministry whether the foreign regulation or policy might be in breach of a WTO obligation. If you have some idea of the nature of the problem, it may help you to read the relevant WTO Agreement. You can get all the Agreements and a lot of explanatory material from the WTO website. They aren't very entertaining to read, but they're not written in very difficult language and many of them are short, considering the complexity of the issues they cover.

(3) Try to find out as much as you can about the origins and effects of the regulations that are causing problems. The more you know about them and their effects, the more likely you are to be able to support your government's efforts on your behalf. Ask your commercial agent in the country (if you have one) to give you some background on the regulations. Ask your own Chamber of Commerce if they have any information from other firms. Be sure to get copies of the regulations. See if you can find more information in the financial press of the country concerned. Many government agencies also maintain web-sites where they detail the regulations that they administer. You may be able to find a great deal of information from the websites belonging to agencies of the foreign government. Use the Internet search engines, too. You should also read the WTO's TPRM (Trade Policy Review Mechanism) reports for the country concerned. You can download these reports from the WTO website. They can often help you understand what is going on in the economy of the country and why the regulations might be the way they are.

(4) Give your own government officials as much information as you can about the nature of the regulation and the size of the problem in financial terms. It's not essential to have a 'legal' interest in order to bring a complaint in the WTO against a regulation which breaches an Agreement, but it certainly helps to convince your own government to take up the case if you can show loss of sales, loss of growth opportunities or increased costs due to the regulation.

(5) Decide what you want. Do you want the regulation changed in some way? Replaced? With what? Remember that the WTO does not tell govern-ments that lose a case precisely what they must do to restore compliance with the covered Agreements. So you can't *always* be certain about the changes that will be made to foreign regulations if you win. You need to take account of the possibility that the foreign government might replace the regulation with another that could be equally bad from your point of view, although consistent with the WTO Agreements. It can be a good idea to try to establish your own contacts with the foreign government, either directly with foreign government officials or through an industry association. These contacts may provide you with information on the intentions of the foreign government if they lose the case. This contact can be very useful, too, at the consultations stage of a case and right up to the final Panel report, when both sides still have the option of reach-ing a 'mutual agreement'. WTO cases are not intended to be 'contentious' and there is no legal impediment – from the WTO's viewpoint – to your contact with the foreign officials. It is certainly worth considering.

(6) If you are hoping for restoration of past commercial losses, or compen-sation for the time and effort you have to put into preparing a case, then forget about a WTO complaint. The WTO does not require governments to offer any compensation for actions that they took prior to the decision in a case – much less for the costs of bringing a case – and only rarely authorizes compensation for continuing trade problems. Furthermore, any compensation offered will be

in the form of market opportunities that will probably benefit other industries or other countries (including your competitors).

7. Think about time and resources carefully. From the time of the first request for consultations until implementation of a decision by the DSB, cases have taken up to 30 months to move through the WTO. You can add another few months to the 'front end' of that for preparation of the case and information collection. Do you have a sufficiently large stake in this to pursue the case given that you'll have to put executive time and effort into working with your own government and, probably, helping them to collect information? Remembering that a 'win' will probably help your competitors just as much as you. Shouldn't you see if your industry association or chamber of commerce will take on the task of working through this case with the government?

You are a government

The DSU requires every Member to 'exercise its judgment as to whether action under these procedures would be fruitful' (Article 3.7). Note the use of the term 'fruitful'. The DSU does not say: 'consider whether you'll win'. Being in a position to 'win' a case may not be sufficient reason to start a dispute settlement process. The following are some questions that should certainly be considered as part of making a judgment about whether dispute settlement action would be 'fruitful'.

(i) Has there been a breach of obligation?

There need not be: the Appellate Body has read the right of Members to bring a case very broadly (see next question). But most cases concern a measure that is inconsistent with a provision of a covered Agreement. This allegation must be substantiated, but once that has been done it establishes a prima facie case of nullification and impairment, creating a presumption in favor of the complainant. No case of 'pure' non-violation impairment – unassociated with any tariff obligation, for example – has succeeded although there have been some cases in GATT that were never adopted (e.g. Japan – Nullification and Impairment of Benefits L/5479).

(ii) Does there need to be a trade interest?

No, the Appellate Body has confirmed (in the EC – Bananas case WT/DS37/ AB/R at 133–135) that there is no need for a Member to have a 'legal interest' in a case in order to bring a dispute. In the Banana case, for example, the USA was found to have the right to bring a case although it did not export bananas to Europe. In that case, too, the potential effect of the European measures on the US future opportunities or on prices in the US domestic market was considered a plausible basis for its interest.

The Appellate Body has read the rights of Members to bring a case in the first paragraph of Article XXIII of GATT 1994 very broadly, suggesting that the 'self-regulating' requirements of DSU Article 3.7 may be the only relevant restraint. However, in the absence of a trade interest it becomes much more difficult to determine whether the expense and inevitable foreign-relations cost of a case is justified by the opportunities that could be opened up by success. Also the Appellate Body has been critical of any lack of 'good faith' in the disputes process; a case that is merely litigious may be given short shrift.

(iii) Is there a 'non-violation' case to answer?

Be careful of 'non-violation' complaints. Few have succeeded under GATT and none under WTO. All successful GATT cases have been associated with breaches of obligations in the tariff schedules. The evidentiary burden on a Member bringing a non-violation complaint is apparently much greater than in the case of a violation complaint. Article 26 of the DSU embodies GATT practice in requiring 'detailed justification in support of any complaint relating to a measure which does not conflict with the relevant covered agreement'. What evidence is needed? In the case of a non-violation measure associated with a tariff obligation or, we could speculate, a GATS scheduled concession or a TRIPS obligation, the GATT jurisprudence (EC – Oilseeds and Norway – Sardines are the classic GATT references) suggests that the complainant must show that the measure could not have been reasonably anticipated and that it in some way upset the competitive position of exports from the complainant country. These matters were again considered by the Panel in Japan – Photographic Film (WT/DS44) and by the Appellate Body in India – Patent Protection (WT/DS50).

(iv) Is there a process in the covered Agreement?

Several of the most important WTO Agreements have special rules and procedures related to disputes that prevail over rules and procedures in the DSU (Article 1.2). In the case of breaches of Agreements such as that on Textiles and Clothing or Subsidies and Countervailing Measures, Anti-Dumping etc, the procedures in the Agreement should be implemented first.

(v) Do previous cases clarify WTO obligations?

Yes. The general rule is that no decision of the DSB – much less a Panel or Appellate Body recommendation – can interpret the Agreements but can only clarify their application in a particular case. So there are no 'rules of precedent' in the WTO. However, adopted Panel reports under the WTO or under the GATT do affect Members' expectations and provide guidance for Panels. Even un-adopted GATT Panel reports may contain helpful reasoning on particular points. In the construction of a case it is essential to check the history of similar issues in earlier Panel reports. Although they may not be 'relied upon' in the same sense as a precedent in a common law jurisdiction, they are nevertheless influential. Supportive 'precedent' strengthens a case.

(vi) Are you 'vulnerable' as a plaintiff?

The DSU specifies that dispute settlement is not a 'contentious' matter and that '... it is also understood that complaints and counter-complaints in regard to distinct matters should not be linked,' (Article 3.10). Some commentators have pointed out, however, that it is difficult to avoid the conclusion that 'counter-claims' on distinct matters are being used as 'leverage'. Whatever the truth of this matter, it would be prudent as a matter of course – and consistent with the DSU's requirement for openness and good faith in the dispute settlement process – to consider whether the respondent might not have some complaints about your own measures. This might, in fact, open up avenues for exchange and mutual agreement that could avoid a dispute altogether.

(vii) How does intervention by other parties affect a dispute?

Members may join together as complainants or may notify their 'substantial interest' in the matter of a dispute to the DSB in order to protect their 'third party' rights (Article 10 of the DSU). The intervention of interested 'third parties' does not seem to promise any advantage to either side in a dispute. There may, however, be some advantage for multiple complainants in a case. Multiple complainants must have the same claims – related to the same Agreements – but may have quite different arguments and factual cases to advance in support of their claims. This may broaden the base of attack on a measure that is said to violate an Agreement, potentially improving the chances of success since only one violation case need succeed before the Panel must recommend withdrawal of the measure. Multiple complainants may also have more success at the consultations stage in persuading the respondent to accept a mutually agreed solution. This may be due to difficulties (and expense) anticipated by the respondent in answering multiple arguments in support of nullification or impairment of rights. But it may also be due to foreign policy considerations: despite the absence of 'contention' in dispute settlement cases, every dispute has potentially adverse effects on a bilateral relationship. Faced with multiple complainants, a respondent is more likely to wish to deal with the problem quickly.

(viii) Is it realistic to expect commercial benefit or relief?

No. As a rule, the commercial interests behind a dispute can usually find other, more direct, means to resolve or manage their problems such as contract arbitration or risk management. Although the timetable for the resolution of disputes is now much tighter than it was under the GATT, the length of time it takes to complete a case – often more than two years from the request for consultations to the implementation of a decision, plus many months of preparation – makes the WTO dispute settlement system unsuitable for most commercial purposes. Also, it must be remembered, that:

- There is no guarantee about the outcome: other than that a violation must be corrected. *How* it is corrected is usually a matter for the respondent government to decide.
- There is no provision for restitution of 'losses' from measures found to violate the Agreements.
- Compensation when granted on a temporary basis is likely to provide trade opportunities for firms in sectors other than the sector where the offending measures are found.

The main exceptions to the 'rule' that WTO cases are unlikely to provide commercial benefit or relief are cases bought under the accelerated disputes procedures under the Agreement on Subsidies and Countervailing Measures and cases where the commercial opportunities denied or frustrated by an inconsistent government measure are specifically due to the measure and so great as to warrant the investment of time and effort by a firm or industry association to support a government case.

(ix) How long will it take?

From first beginning to put a case together to final implementation of a recommendation to withdraw an inconsistent measure can easily take from two to three years, particularly where developing countries are involved, because the DSU affords developing countries more time to prepare and respond to a case. See Table 4 (above) for the formal timetable.

(x) How much will it cost?

That depends a lot on the case. As a guide, it probably costs a plaintiff government and businesses in the plaintiff country several millions of dollars over three years (or so), if all costs are taken into account.

A Member government will probably need to dedicate one or two professional staff full time to the development and prosecution of a WTO case with associated administrative and support costs. Senior officials and Ministers will have to be available for supervision and to make key decisions. Agencies and Ministries in the Capital whose portfolios and responsibilities may be affected by the decisions in a case will need to be consulted and there will be information costs associated with data collection – including from business, statistical sources and from foreign sources.

External legal advisors are likely to be very expensive, if used. The use of a law firm to draft or advise on a case is not necessary and may not convey a great advantage on a complainant or respondent. The use of representatives – whether officials or not – with legal training and experience is necessary in an Appeal, where the issues to be considered are matters of law and legal interpretation.

The participants in a case will need to ensure representation in Geneva (and possibly elsewhere) during the preliminary phases including the formal consultation phase. They will certainly need to be represented at the DSB meetings before and after the establishment of a Panel and during the decision and implementation phases of the case. They will also need to have representatives appear before the Panel on two occasions and before the Appellate Body, if an appeal is made.

Businesses in the Member states will also need to consult with government agencies and may participate in the evaluation of the case or give advice to their government on the progress of implementation.

(xi) What are the alternatives to Dispute Settlement?

The first alternative is to avoid a formal dispute. It's less costly and frequently more effective to resolve matters bilaterally without resort to the WTO dispute settlement system at all. Many disputes are quickly resolved on a bilateral basis without resort to formal dispute settlement processes: although the *alternative of formal adjudication* sometimes brings one side or the other to agree more quickly on an informal bilateral settlement (see text box).

In some cases, governments may be parties to other multilateral or bilateral regional trade agreements that contain disputes mechanisms – such as the disputes panels created by the North American Free Trade Agreement. These disputes mechanisms can complement WTO dispute settlement. In some cases, too, governments may be parties to commercial contracts where disputes can be adjudicated by, for example, the International Chamber of Commerce. But there is no formal alternative to WTO dispute settlement for the resolution of differences *under the WTO Agreements*.

Disputes procedure avoids 'trade war'

United States – Imposition of Import Duties on Automobiles from Japan ... was one of such cases where the parties reached a mutually satisfactory solution. Faced with a stalemate in the bilateral negotiations with Japan over access to the Japanese automobiles and auto parts market, the United States announced on 16 May 1995 its intention to impose a 100 per cent tariff on Japanese luxury cars as of 28 June 1995. Japan requested urgent consultations pursuant to the DSU, alleging that the United States violated, inter alia, GATT Articles I and II. Separately, the

United States indicated its intention to request consultations with Japan over the auto and auto parts issue under the DSU. On 28 June 1995, Japan and the United States reached an agreement on the auto and auto parts issue, and the United States withdrew its announcement of the 100 per cent tariff. WTO Director-General Renato Ruggiero remarked, 'the **WTO dispute settlement system has done its job as a deterrent against conflict and a promoter of an agreement**. The knowledge that both sides were prepared to use the system played a crucial role in pressing them towards a deal.' *WTO Annual Report, 1996 (emphasis added)*

(xii) Is 'unilateral action' an option?

No. Article 23 of the DSU specifically prohibits any decisions on the nullification or impairment of benefits under the WTO Agreements except through the DSU procedures. Members undertake to make no decision, either, on the 'reasonable period of time' for implementation of a DSB decision or on the level of concessions that could be suspended in retaliation or sought in compensation as the result of a DSB decision, *except* through the normal WTO dispute settlement system procedures. This means that Members have undertaken not to use national processes or laws such as the United States' Trade Act Section 301 to make such decisions.

One of the most unusual cases so far considered in the WTO dispute settlement system concerned the possibility of unilateral action. This was a *violation* case in which there was no actual *measure* identified by the complainant. In *United States – Sections 301–310 of the Trade Act*, the European Communities (WT/DS152) claimed that merely the *threat* of unilateral measures constituted a *prima facie* case of nullification and impairment of the benefits of the Agreements – specifically of the benefits of the DSU. The Panel agreed with this claim saying,

> Merely carrying a big stick is, in many cases, as effective a means to having one's way as actually using the stick … The threat of unilateral action can be as damaging on the market-place as the action itself.

However the Panel found that there was, in fact, no violation by the USA because statements by the US Administration adopted by Congress and confirmed by US undertakings before the Panel demonstrated that the Administration's mandate to take unilateral action in a WTO dispute before DSU procedures were exhausted had been curtailed. The DSB adopted the Panel report, which was not appealed.

(xiii) Should you consider conciliation or mediation?

Definitely. Conciliation appears to have been an underused facility of the DSU. This may well be because, as several commentators have pointed out, it is a 'diplomatic' procedure that is at odds with the 'litigious' attitude of Members armed with detailed WTO 'legal' cases. Although the Appellate Body has gone on record strongly criticizing the litigious approach to the resolution of disputes, there seems no doubt that the increasing legalism of the WTO dispute settlement system has promoted the desire to 'win' rather than to resolve a dispute.

Although there is little evidence of its formal use to date under Article 5 of the DSU, conciliation and mediation is available to the Parties right up to the point of the final Panel report. It is likely that some degree of informal concili- ation and mediation takes place in many disputes, by the WTO Secretariat, at the level of the DSB or by the Chairmen of the Committees of the covered Agreements when disputes first arise. Informal conciliation or mediation may explain, in part, the number of notified disputes that do not proceed to a Panel.

Conciliation may be most valuable to the complainant if it appears that the legal case for the complaint is faulty or the facts are uncertain or the respondent appears willing to be flexible but unwilling to make a simple concession. Sometimes Members may need to find external motives – such as the interven- tion of the Director-General – for making a concession in order to counter domestic political pressures to 'stay the course'.

Conciliation and mediation should be considered in every case involving a measure maintained by a least-developed country.

(xiv) Is independent legal advice a good idea?

Most Members now use legal services – either internal or external – to assist with the preparation or review of a case. Also, the Appellate Body has encour- aged governments to appoint representatives at Appellate hearings that have legal training because the appellate process is focused on legal interpretations.

The drafters of the DSU were apparently mindful of the greater need for legal representation when they required the WTO Secretariat (in Article 27) to make at least one qualified lawyer available to assist developing countries. The Secretariat has provided two part-time legal positions, filled by external appoint- ments, for this purpose. But the rush of WTO dispute settlement cases and the strong role played by the Appellate Body quickly resulted in a greater demand for legal advice. At the initiative of some developed-country Members, an exter- nal organization was created that could offer what the WTO could not: 'parti- san' legal assistance for developing countries in WTO disputes. The Advisory Centre on WTO Law (see text box) is expected to begin operations in mid-2001.

Independent legal advice on WTO trade law can be very expensive. In part this is because there is a limited community of international lawyers with trade experience and most of them are practicing in lucrative developed-country mar- kets. Also the Parties' submissions in cases where law firms are given responsi- bility for the drafting are increasingly swelled by an exhaustive review of the facts and a detailed exploration of legal claims – some or even many of which may be included as 'insurance' in case they are considered germane by the Panel. Charges for these monumental submissions are correspondingly great.

The Advisory Centre on WTO Law

The Centre was established in 1999 by 32 WTO member countries (nine developed and 23 developing) as a 'law office' specialized in WTO law, that can provide legal services and training exclusively to developing countries and economies in transition. It is expected to begin operations in mid-2001 once its funding is complete.

Functions: The Centre's mandate and modest size (one Executive Director, four experienced lawyers and support staff) require the Centre to stay within its own niche, to avoid overlap and to complement the training and technical cooperation provided by the WTO Secretariat and other relevant institutions. The Centre will organize seminars on WTO jurisprudence and provide legal advice. Internships will be opened for government officials from developing country Members and Least-Developed Countries (LDCs). The Centre will also provide support throughout dispute settlement proceedings in the WTO at discounted rates for its Members and LDCs in accordance with the terms set out in annex IV of the Agreement.

Financing: Members from developing countries and economies in transition pay a one-time financial contribution (in accordance with their capacity to pay) to an endowment fund that forms the financial core of the Centre. LDCs are not required to make such payments to enjoy all the benefits and will furthermore receive priority in the provision of the Centre's services. Developed countries can become Members by making a minimum contribution of US$1,000,000 to the endowment fund and/or by donating multiyear funds of US$1,250,000. Developed countries have no access to the legal services in dispute settlement proceedings.

For more information: *http://www.itd.org/links/acwlintro.htm*

In its current configuration, the successful management of a WTO dispute settlement case appears to require both diplomatic and legal contributions. The application of legal reasoning to the factual situation of a WTO case can greatly improve the strength and completeness of the arguments advanced by the Parties. But it is not necessary to have formal legal qualifications in order to draft or present a case and legal skills are usually not sufficient, on their own, to conduct a successful case. Trade administrators, who have experience of the WTO disputes system and who understand the business or community needs and expectations that lie behind a dispute, are usually needed too.

The lawyers may help to 'win' a case that goes to a Panel and/or to the Appellate Body, but diplomatic contributions may well keep the case 'out of court' or help to win a quick resolution based on mutually agreed implementation options.

(xv) Who may represent a Member?

Whomever the Member decides, says the Appellate Body. Specifically, Members may be represented before the Panels or the Appellate Body by non-government legal advisors, if they so choose

> We note that there are no provisions in the *Marrakesh Agreement Establishing the World Trade Organization* (the "*WTO Agreement*"), in the DSU or in the *Working Procedures* that specify who can represent a government in making its representations in an oral hearing of the Appellate Body. With respect to GATT practice, we can find no previous panel report which speaks specifically to this issue in the context of panel meetings with the parties. We also note that representation by counsel of a government's own choice may well be a matter of particular significance – especially for developing-country Members – to enable them to participate fully in dispute settlement proceedings. Moreover, given the Appellate Body's mandate to review only issues of law or legal interpretation in panel reports, it is particularly important that governments be represented by qualified counsel in Appellate Body proceedings.
>
> *EC-Bananas (WT/DS27/AB/R at 12)*

Chapter Five
Disputes by subject

To understand the WTO dispute settlement system, there is no substitute for reading at least the summaries of the Panel reports and especially the reports of the Appellate Body.

The Panel reports themselves frequently review the submissions at length and may be best read in extract by non-specialists. The brief summaries of the Panel reports provided by the WTO Secretariat in the WTO Annual Reports or in the 'State of Play' document that can be downloaded from the 'Disputes' section of the WTO website are an invaluable guide to the main questions considered by the Panels and the views and recommendations contained in the Panel reports. You should consider reading these first of all.

Appellate Body reports – like the Panel reports – can be downloaded from the WTO 'on-line documents' facility. The document number is the same as the Panel report number (see table below) with the extension '/AB/R'. Appellate Body reports, too, are summarized in the WTO Secretariat's 'State of Play' document and in the Annual Reports, but they are sufficiently authoritative – and not sufficiently short – to repay reading in the original.

Cases adjudicated to January 2001[#]

Short Title	Panel Document	Complainant	Main Issues*
Argentina – Certain Measures Affecting Imports of Footwear	WT/DS56	USA	Customs, schedules
Argentina – Measures Affecting the Export of Bovine Hides	WT/DS155	EC	Quotas, National treatment
Argentina – Safeguard Measures on Imports of Footwear	WT/DS121	EC	Safeguards
Australia – Measures Affecting the Importation of Salmon	WT/DS18	Canada	Sanitary and phytosanitary
Australia – Subsidies Provided to Producers of Leather	WT/DS126	USA	Subsidies and countervailing measures
Brazil – Export Financing Programme for Aircraft	WT/DS46	Canada	Subsidies and countervailing measures
Brazil – Measures Affecting Desiccated Coconut		Philippines	Subsidies and countervailing measures

[#] Not all cases related to the same matter are listed.
* Please note that 'main issues' is an informal description of the main claims. It is not a complete description.

Cases adjudicated to January 2001# *cont'd*

Short Title	Panel Document	Complainant	Main Issues*
Canada – Certain Measures Affecting the Automotive Industry	WT/DS139 and WT/DS142	EC, Japan	MFN, Subsidies and countervailing measures, services, National treatment, Article XXIV of GATT
Canada – Patent Protection of Pharmaceutical Products	WT/DS114	EC	Intellectual property
Canada – Term of Patent Protection, Complaint by …	WT/DS170	USA	Intellectual property
Canada – Certain Measures Concerning Periodicals		USA	Quota, National treatment
Canada – Measures Affecting the Export of Civilian Aircraft	WT/DS70	Brazil	Subsidies and countervailing measures
Canada – Measures Affecting the Importation of Milk	WT/DS103	USA, New Zealand	Schedules, agriculture
Chile – Taxes on Alcoholic Beverages	WT/DS87 and 110	EC	National treatment
European Communities – Customs Classification	WT/DS62 WT/DS67 WT/DS68	USA	Customs, Schedules, Legitimate expectations
EC – Trade Description Scallops	WT/DS7/R	Canada	Schedules
European Communities – Measures Affecting Meat (Hormones)	WT/DS26 WT/DS48	USA	Sanitary and phytosanitary
European Communities – Regime for Bananas	WT/DS27	USA, Ecuador, Guatemala, Honduras	MFN, Services, Quota, National treatment, Schedules
Guatemala – Definitive Anti-Dumping Measures on Cement	WT/DS156	Mexico	Anti-dumping
Guatemala – Anti-Dumping Investigation Regarding Imports of Portland Cement	WT/DS60	Mexico	Anti-dumping
India – Patent Protection for Pharmaceutical Products	WT/DS50	USA	Intellectual property, Legitimate expectations, Non-violation
India – Patent Protection for Pharmaceutical Products	WT/DS79	EC	Intellectual property
India – Quantitative Restrictions on Imports	WT/DS90	USA	Quota, BOP
Indonesia – Certain Measures Affecting the Automobile Industry	WT/DS54 WT/DS55 WT/DS59 WT/DS64	EC, Japan	MFN, Subsidies and countervailing measures, National treatment, TRIMS
Japan – Alcoholic Beverages		USA	National treatment
Japan – Measures Affecting Agricultural Products	WT/DS76	USA	Sanitary and phytosanitary
Japan – Measures Affecting Consumer Photographic Film	WT/DS44	USA	National treatment, Non-violation

Cases adjudicated to January 2001# *cont'd*

Short Title	Panel Document	Complainant	Main Issues*
Korea – Definitive Safeguard Measure on Imports of Certain Dairy Products	WT/DS98	EC	Safeguard
Korea – Measures Affecting Government Procurement	WT/DS163	USA	Non-violation, Government Procurement
Korea – Measures Affecting Imports of Fresh, Chilled and Frozen Beef	WT/DS/161 and 169	USA, Australia	Quota, National treatment, Schedules, Agriculture, Import Licensing
Korea – Definitive Safeguard Measure on Imports of Certain Dairy Products	WT/DS98	EC	Safeguards
Korea – Taxes on Alcoholic Beverages	WT/DS75 WT/DS84	USA, EC	National treatment
Mexico – Anti-Dumping Investigation of High-Fructose Corn Syrup	WT/DS132	USA	Anti-dumping
Turkey – Restrictions on Imports of Textile and Clothing	WT/DS34	India	Textiles and clothing, Quotas, Article XXIV of GATT
United States – Anti-Dumping Act of 1916	WT/DS136 WT/DS162	EC, Japan	Anti-dumping, National treatment
United States – Anti-Dumping Measures on Stainless Steel Plate	WT/DS179	Korea	Anti-dumping
United States – Definitive Safeguard Measures Wheat Gluten	WT/DS166	EC	Agriculture, safeguard
United States – Import Measures on Certain Products	WT/DS165	EC	MFN, schedules, DSU
United States – Imposition of Countervailing Duties	WT/DS138	EC	Subsidies and countervailing measures
United States – Measures Affecting Wool Shirts and Blouses		India	Textiles and clothing
United States – Reformulated Gasoline		Venezuela	National treatment
United States – Section 110(5) of US Copyright Act	WT/DS160	EC	Intellectual property
United States – Tax Treatment for "Foreign Sales…	WT/DS108	EC	Subsidies and countervailing measures, National treatment
United States – Anti-Dumping Duty on Dynamic Random	WT/DS99	Korea	Anti-dumping
United States – Import Prohibition of Certain Shrimp and Shrimp Products	WT/DS58	India, Malaysia, Pakistan, Thailand	Quotas, 'environment', Article XX
United States – Sections 301–310 of the Trade Act of	WT/DS152	EC	DSU
US – Restrictions on Imports of Cotton and Man-Made		Costa Rica	Textiles and clothing

In preparing a complaint or a response, you should read through the reports of the Panel and the Appellate Body on the Agreement(s) that are listed in the complaint (the table above and the 'state of play' document will help you to identify the cases). If, however, your interest is in learning more about the WTO and the dispute settlement system then you might consider reading at least the Panel report summaries and scanning the Appellate Body reports on some of the following selection of WTO cases.

(i) DSU Procedures

US – Reformulated Gasoline and **Japan – Alcohol** (Appellate Body report): rules of interpretation and procedure for the Panels and Appellate Body including the use of the Vienna Convention and the additional rules of interpretation.

EC – Bananas and **Korea – Dairy Products** (Appellate Body reports): rules of procedure for complaints particularly requirements affecting the request for a panel; rules concerning representation before the Panel or Appellate Body; a Member does not need to demonstrate a 'legal interest' in order to bring a complaint.

US – Import measures on certain products (Appellate Body report): right to interpret the DSU rests with Members; retaliation for non-implementation may not precede the determination of the inconsistency of implementing measures.

EC – Hormones (Appellate Body report): mere errors of judgment do not void a Panel's 'objective assessment of the facts.' A panel does not need to examine the facts of a case 'de novo' (i.e. 'starting from the beginning') in order to meet the required standard of review.

India – Patents on pharmaceutical products (Appellate Body report): a panel may consider only those claims it has the authority to consider under its Terms of Reference.

US – FSC (Appellate Body report): litigious behavior may not meet the test of 'good faith' required by the DSU and may lead to the failure of a claim.

India – Quantitative restrictions on imports of agricultural equipment (Appellate Body report): Use of expert evidence.

United States – Woven shirts (Appellate Body report): burden of proof falls in general on the party making the positive assertion.

(ii) Safeguards

Korea – Dairy Safeguards: a Member may be required to apply both GATT (1947) and other WTO disciplines where these are relevant and not specifically inconsistent.

(iii) SPS

EC – Hormones: The risk that is to be evaluated in a risk assessment under Article 5.1 is not only risk ascertainable in a science laboratory operating under strict controlled conditions, but also risk in human societies as they actually exist. The evidentiary burden of proof in an SPS case does not lie only with the country maintaining the measure: it is first up to the complainants to establish a *prima facie* case of the inconsistency of an SPS measure with the SPS Agreement.

Australia – Salmon: Requirement for risk assessment and the nature of arbitrary and unjustifiable distinctions between imported products that amount to disguised restriction on trade.

(iv) TRIMS

Indonesia – Measures affecting the automobile industry: local content laws violate the TRIMS agreement.

(v) Non-violation complaints

India – Pharmaceutical Patents (Complaint by the USA): clarifies the 'legitimate expectations' that may be impaired by non-violating measures.

(vi) Intellectual Property

India – Pharmaceutical Patents (USA and EC complaints)
    Canada – Term of Patent Protection

(vii) Textiles and Clothing

US – Cotton and man-made fiber underwear (complaint by Costa Rica): requirement of the ATC agreement that safeguards be imposed only after serious damage is demonstrated to be due to imports.

(viii) 'Environment'

US – Import prohibition on certain shrimp: The general exceptions in Article XX do apply to the conservation of the natural environment and may permit a wide range of measures inconsistent with other obligations of the Agreements as long as these measures conform to the provisions of the preambular requirements of Article XX.

(ix) National treatment

Chile – Taxes on alcoholic beverages (Appellate Body report): National treatment requires equality of competitive conditions for all directly competitive or substitutable imported products in relation to domestic products, and not simply for some of these imported products (as defined by, e.g. fiscal categories).

    EC – Bananas: National treatment under GATS article II.

(x) Export subsidies

Canada – Measures affecting the export of civilian aircraft: The 'benefit' that characterizes an export subsidy is not necessarily to be determined by the 'cost to government' of a 'financial contribution', but may also be determined to be the benefit to the recipient of that contribution. A 'benefit' is conferred when 'the recipient has received a 'financial contribution' on terms more favourable than those available to the recipient in a competitive market.'

United States – Imposition of Countervailing Duties on lead and bismuth carbon steel products: an investigation authority conducting a review of countervailing duties must determine, in the light of all the facts before it, whether there is a continuing need for the application of these duties.

United States – Tax treatment for 'Foreign Sales Corporations': application of a tax subsidy measure, in a manner which results in, or threatens to lead to, circumvention of its export subsidy commitments with respect to agricultural products under Articles 10.1 and 8 of the Agreement on Agriculture.

Australia – Subsidies provided to producers and exporters of automotive leather: in some cases, only full repayment of the subsidy would enable the recommendation to withdraw to operate as an effective remedy for having granted a prohibited subsidy in violation of the SCM Agreement.

(xi) Anti-dumping

Guatemala – Definitive anti-dumping measures on Portland cement: standards for investigation of an anti-dumping claim including the conduct of the investigation and the respondent's rights of due process.

United States – Anti-dumping Act of 1916: GATT Article VI and the WTO AD Agreement apply to any action taken in response to situations involving 'dumping', as that concept is defined in WTO law. Inconsistent measures may not be justified by reference to (pre-existing) legislation inconsistent with those agreements.

Mexico – Anti-dumping investigation of high-fructose corn syrup: Each of the injury factors set forth in the Anti-Dumping Agreement must be specifically addressed in an investigation. Specifically, a positive finding on the threat of injury must be assessed by reference to the entire domestic industry, and not only that portion of it that directly competes with imports.

Remember, too, that GATT cases – both those where the Panel report was adopted and some of those where it was not adopted – may also be relevant. You will find references to some key reports in the WTO Panel reports. You can also download the adopted GATT Panel reports from the WTO website (disputes section).

Annex I
Dispute Settlement Body (DSB), Annual Report (2000)

The following annex sets out the actions taken by the Dispute Settlement Body (DSB) during 2000. For more recent developments you should consult the WTO's website at http://www.wto.org/english/tratop_e/dispu_e/dispu_e.htm and in particular the document prepared by the Secretariat entitled 'Update Of WTO Dispute Settlement Cases' which is updated several times a year.

Dispute Settlement Body
Annual Report (2000)[1]

The present report has been prepared in pursuance of the Procedures for an Annual Overview of WTO Activities and for Reporting under the WTO (WT/L/105), and sets out the actions taken by the Dispute Settlement Body (DSB) in the period since its previous annual report.[2]

In carrying out its task, the DSB has held 23 meetings since the period covered by the previous report. The minutes of these meetings, which remain the record of the DSB's work, are contained in documents WT/DSB/M/70–WT/DSB/M/92.[3]

The following subjects are included in the report:

---

[1] The Overview of the State of Play of WTO Disputes since 1 January 1995 to 31 October 2000 prepared by the Secretariat on its own responsibility is included, for practical purposes, in an Addendum to this report.
[2] WT/DSB/16, Corr.1 and Add.1.
[3] The present report includes meetings of the DSB covering the period from 27 October 1999 to 17 November 2000.

1. Election of Chairperson (WT/DSB/M/76)

At its meeting on *24 February 2000*, the DSB elected Mr. Stuart Harbinson (Hong Kong, China) as Chairman by acclamation.

The representatives of the European Communities, United States, India, Thailand (on behalf of the ASEAN Members), Japan, Costa Rica (on behalf of Latin American and Caribbean Members), the outgoing Chairman and the incoming Chairman spoke.

The DSB took note of the statements.

2. Review of the DSU (WT/DSB/M/70, 72)

At the DSB meeting on *27 October 1999*, Mr. Suzuki (Japan), who had chaired informal discussions on the DSU review reported, in his personal capacity, on the progress made thus far.

The representatives of Mexico, European Communities, Malaysia, Egypt, Venezuela, Colombia, Canada, Costa Rica, Turkey, Brazil, Switzerland, Norway, New Zealand, Korea, India, Ecuador, Guatemala, Argentina, Hungary, Indonesia, Thailand, Australia, United States, Philippines and Hong Kong, China and the Chairman spoke.

The DSB took note of the statements and agreed to revert to this matter at its resumed meeting on 3 November 1999.

Upon resumption of the DSB meeting on *3 November 1999*, the Chairman presented his statement, prepared on the basis of the discussion held on 27 October 1999, to be read out, on his own responsibility, at the meeting of the General Council on 4 November 1999.

The representatives of the Philippines, United States, Malaysia, Mexico, Venezuela, Ecuador, Indonesia, Egypt and Hong Kong, China and the Chairman spoke.

The DSB took note of the statements.

At the DSB meeting on *9 December 1999*, the representative of Uruguay recalled that no decision on the DSU review had been taken at the Third Session of the Ministerial Conference in Seattle. He therefore believed that it would be appropriate for the General Council to take a decision to continue with the current DSU, in accordance with the 1994 Ministerial Decision.

The representatives of Uruguay, United States, Philippines and the European Communities spoke.

The DSB took note of the statements.

3. Appointment of Appellate Body members (WT/DSB/M/70, 74, 75, 76, 77, 78, 82)

At its meeting on *27 October and 3 November 1999*, the Chairman proposed that the DSB agree: (i) to renew the terms of Messrs. Bacchus and Beeby for a final term of four years; (ii) to commence a process to ensure the rapid replacement of two Appellate Body members who had expressed their desire to leave, following the process used in 1995 to select the original seven Appellate Body members, which would involve nominations by WTO Members by 17 December 1999, and the establishment of a Selection Committee composed of the Director-General together with the 1999 Chairs of the General Council, the DSB, and the Councils for Trade in Goods, Services and TRIPS, with a view to a recommendation being made to the DSB for a decision at its meeting in March 2000; and (iii) to extend the terms of Messrs. El-Naggar and Matsushita until the end of March 2000.

The representatives of Brazil, India, Australia, Mexico, Malaysia, Japan, Canada and the Chairman spoke.

The DSB took note of the statements and agreed to the proposal outlined by the Chairman.

At the DSB meeting on *27 January 2000*, the Chairman proposed that the deadline of 17 December 1999 for submission of candidates for the Appellate Body members be extended until 17 February 2000.

The representatives of Japan, Canada, United States, Slovenia and the Chairman spoke.

The DSB took note of the statements and agreed to extend the deadline for submission of candidates for the Appellate Body members until 17 February 2000.

At the DSB meeting on *11 February 2000*, the Chairman informed the DSB that the Selection Committee would start interviews of candidates in the week of 28 February 2000.

The DSB took note of the statement.

At the DSB meeting on *24 February 2000*, the Chairman made a statement concerning the selection process for the Appellate Body members.

The representative of Thailand spoke.

The DSB took note of the statements.

At the DSB meeting on *20 March 2000*, the Chairman reported on the work of the Selection Committee thus far. He noted that it was the intention of the Committee to take a decision on this matter before the next regular meeting of the DSB or at a special meeting to be convened for that purpose shortly thereafter.

The DSB took note of the statement.

At the DSB meeting on *7 April 2000*, the Chairman read out a statement conveying the Selection Committee's recommendations to appoint Messrs. Abi Saab and Ganesan as members of the Appellate Body for four years from a date, to be fixed in the near future, on which their contracts would commence. He proposed that the DSB agree to the recommendations of the Selection Committee.

The DSB so agreed.

The Chairman also proposed that the DSB authorize the Selection Committee to continue its work in relation to the selection of an additional candidate to fill the vacancy left by the late Mr. Beeby and that the DSB agree to invite Members wishing to submit or resubmit candidates for this third vacancy to do so no later than 5 May 2000.

The DSB agreed to the Chairman's proposal.

The representatives of Egypt, Japan, Philippines (on behalf of the ASEAN Members), Israel, Poland (on behalf of CEFTA Members and Estonia and Latvia), European Communities, United States, India, Mexico, Australia, Canada and the Chairman spoke.

The DSB took note of the statements.

At the DSB meeting on *25 May 2000*, the Chairman read out the statement conveying the Selection Committee's recommendation to appoint Mr. Taniguchi as a member of the Appellate Body for the remainder of the late Mr. Beeby's term, that was, up to and including 10 December 2003. He proposed that the DSB agree to the recommendation of the Selection Committee.

The DSB so agreed.

The representatives of Japan, Australia, United States, Bulgaria, European Communities and the Chairman spoke.

The DSB took note of the statements.

4. Term of appointment of Appellate Body members (WT/DSB/M/71)

At the DSB meeting on *19 November 1999*, the representative of India introduced his country's proposal contained in document WT/DSB/W/117 with regard to the term of appointment of Appellate Body members.

The representatives of India, European Communities, Canada, Norway, Mexico, Japan, Switzerland, United States and Hong Kong, China and the Chairman spoke.

The DSB took note of the statements and agreed to revert to this matter at its future meeting.

5. Progress report on informal consultations on the question of harmonization of the terms of office of Appellate Body members and selection processes for future appointments to the Appellate Body (WT/DSB/M/82)

At the DSB on *25 May 2000*, the Chairman reported on the consultations he had held on the question of harmonization of the terms of office of Appellate Body members and selection processes for future appointments to the Appellate Body.

The DSB took note of the statement.

6. Adoption of the 2000 draft Annual Report of the DSB (WT/DSB/M/92)

At the DSB meeting on *17 November 2000*, the Chairman proposed that the DSB adopt its 2000 draft Annual Report contained in WT/DSB/W/147 and Add.1 and Add.1/Corr.1 and authorize the Secretariat to update the Report under its own responsibility in order to include the actions taken by the DSB at the present meeting. He said that the updated Annual Report would be submitted for consideration by the General Council at its meeting on 7 and 8 December 2000.

The representatives of Mexico and the Chairman spoke.

The DSB took note of the statements and adopted the draft Annual Report contained in WT/DSB/W/147 and Add.1 and Add.1/Corr.1.

7. Indicative list of governmental and non-governmental panelists (WT/DSB/M/70, 76, 77, 80, 89, 91)

At its meeting on *27 October and 3 November 1999*, the DSB approved the names contained in document WT/DSB/W/114 proposed for inclusion on the indicative list in accordance with Article 8.4 of the DSU.

At its meeting on *24 February 2000*, the DSB approved the names contained in documents WT/DSB/W/120 and WT/DSB/W/123 proposed for inclusion on the indicative list in accordance with Article 8.4 of the DSU.

At its meeting on *20 March 2000*, the DSB approved the names contained in document WT/DSB/W/126 and Corr.1 proposed for inclusion on the indicative list in accordance with Article 8.4 of the DSU.

At its meeting on *18 May 2000*, the DSB approved the names contained in document WT/DSB/W/130 proposed for inclusion on the indicative list in accordance with Article 8.4 of the DSU.

At its meeting on *26 September 2000*, the DSB approved the names contained in document WT/DSB/W/142 proposed for inclusion on the indicative list in accordance with Article 8.4 of the DSU.

At its meeting on *23 October 2000*, the DSB approved the name contained in document WT/DSB/W/145 proposed for inclusion on the indicative list in accordance with Article 8.4 of the DSU.

8. Chairmanship of a possible DSB meeting in the second half of August (WT/DSB/M/86)

At the DSB meeting on *27 July 2000*, the DSB agreed to appoint the Chairman of the Council for Trade in Goods, Mr. Pérez de Castillo (Uruguay) to chair any DSB meeting that might be required, for reasons of urgency, during the second half of August.

The representative of Panama and the Chairman spoke.

The DSB took note of the statements.

9. Recourse to dispute settlement procedures

(a) Argentina

(i) Definitive anti-dumping measures on carton-board imports from Germany and definitive anti-dumping measures on imports of ceramic floor tiles from Italy (WT/DSB/M/89)

At its meeting on *26 September 2000*, the DSB considered a request by the European Communities for the establishment of a panel to examine its complaint with regard to Argentina's definitive anti-dumping measures on carton-board imports from Germany and on imports of ceramic floor tiles from Italy (WT/DS189/2).

The representatives of the European Communities and Argentina spoke.

The DSB took note of the statements and agreed to revert to this matter.

(ii) Definitive anti-dumping measures on imports of ceramic floor tiles from Italy (WT/DSB/M/92)

At its meeting on *17 November 2000*, the DSB considered a request by the European Communities for the establishment of a panel to examine its complaint with regard to Argentina's anti-dumping measures on imports of ceramic floor tiles from Italy (WT/DS189/3). The Chairman drew attention to the fact that the EC's request had already been considered by the DSB on 26 September 2000 as part of the EC's broader complaint contained in WT/DS189/2.

The representatives of the European Communities and Argentina spoke.

The DSB took note of the statements and agreed to establish a panel in accordance with the provisions of Article 6 of the DSU, with standard terms of reference.

The representatives of Japan, Turkey and the United States reserved their third-party rights to participate in the Panel's proceedings.

(iii) Safeguard measures on imports of footwear (WT/DSB/M/73, 75, 76, 77)

In July 1998,[4] the DSB had established a panel to examine the complaint by the European Communities with regard to Argentina's safeguard measures on imports of footwear. In September 1999, Argentina had notified the DSB of its decision to appeal certain issues of law and legal interpretations developed by the Panel.

At its meeting on *12 January 2000*, the DSB considered the Appellate Body Report contained in WT/DS121/AB/R and the Panel Report contained in WT/DS121/R pertaining to the complaint by the European Communities.

---

[4] WT/DSB/M/47.

The representatives of the European Communities, Argentina, Indonesia, Brazil, United States and Uruguay spoke.

The DSB took note of the statements and adopted the Appellate Body Report in WT/DS121/AB/R and the Panel Report in WT/DS121/R as modified by the Appellate Body Report.

At the DSB meeting on *11 February 2000*, the representative of Argentina informed the DSB of his country's intentions in respect of implementation of the DSB's recommendations on this matter, pursuant to Article 21.3 of the DSU.

The representatives of Argentina, United States, European Communities and Indonesia spoke.

The DSB took note of the statements and of the information provided by Argentina regarding its intentions in respect of implementation of the DSB's recommendations.

At the DSB meeting on *24 February 2000*, the representative of the United States expressed concern about Argentina's intention regarding its safeguard measures on imports of footwear.

The representatives of the United States, Argentina, European Communities and Indonesia spoke.

The DSB took note of the statements.

At the DSB meeting on *20 March 2000*, the representative of the European Communities expressed concern about Argentina's lack of implementation in this case.

The representatives of the European Communities, Indonesia and Argentina spoke.

The DSB took note of the statements.

(iv) Transitional safeguard measures on certain imports of woven fabrics of cotton and cotton mixtures originating in Brazil (WT/DSB/M/76, 77)

At its meeting on *24 February 2000*, the DSB considered a request by Brazil for the establishment of a panel to examine its complaint with regard to transitional safeguard measures imposed by Argentina on certain imports of woven fabrics of cotton and cotton mixtures originating in Brazil (WT/DS190/1).

The representatives of Brazil, Argentina and Pakistan spoke.

The DSB took note of the statements and agreed to revert to this matter.

At the DSB meeting on *20 March 2000*, the DSB again considered this matter.

The representatives of Brazil and Argentina spoke.

The DSB took note of the statements and agreed to establish a panel in accordance with the provisions of Article 6 of the DSU, with standard terms of reference.

The representatives of Pakistan, Paraguay and the United States reserved their third-party rights to participate in the Panel's proceedings.

---

[5] WT/DSB/M/66.

(b) Australia

(i) Measures affecting importation of salmon – Recourse to Article 21.5 of the DSU by Canada (WT/DSB/M/77, 80)

In July 1999,[5] the DSB had agreed, in accordance with Article 21.5 of the DSU, to refer to the original Panel a request by Canada for determination of consistency of the implementation measures in this case.

At its meeting on *20 March 2000*, the DSB considered the Panel Report contained in WT/DS18/RW pertaining to this matter.

The representatives of Canada, Australia, United States, European Communities and Norway spoke.

The DSB took note of the statements and adopted the Panel Report contained in WT/DS18/RW.

At the DSB meeting on *18 May 2000*, Canada and Australia announced that they had reached an agreement on this matter.

The representatives of Canada, Australia, United States and Norway spoke.

The DSB took note of the statements.

(ii) Subsidies provided to producers and exporters of automotive leather – Recourse to Article 21.5 of the DSU by the United States (WT/DSB/M/75)

In October 1999,[6] the DSB had agreed, in accordance with Article 21.5 of the DSU, to refer to the original Panel the matter raised by the United States concerning the measures taken by Australia to comply with the DSB's recommendations in this case.

At its meeting on *11 February 2000*, the DSB considered the Panel Report contained in WT/DS126/RW and Corr.1 pertaining to this matter.

The representatives of the United States, Australia, Canada, Brazil, Japan, European Communities, Malaysia and Hong Kong, China spoke.

The DSB took note of the statements and adopted the Panel Report contained in WT/DS126/RW and Corr.1.

(c) Brazil

(i) Export financing programme for aircraft (WT/DSB/M/71, 72, 81)

At the DSB meeting on *19 November 1999*, the representative of Canada made a statement concerning the implementation by Brazil of the DSB's recommendations on this matter (WT/DS46).

The representatives of Canada and Brazil spoke.

The DSB took note of the statements.

---

[6] WT/DSB/M/69.

At its meeting on *9 December 1999*, the DSB considered a request by Canada under Article 21.5 of the DSU to examine Brazil's implementation of the DSB's recommendations on this matter (WT/DS46/13).

The representatives of Canada and Brazil spoke.

The DSB took note of the statements and agreed to refer to the original Panel, pursuant to Article 21.5 of the DSU, the matter raised by Canada in document WT/DS46/13. It was agreed that the Panel would have standard terms of reference.

The representatives of the European Communities and the United States reserved their third-party rights to participate in the Panel's proceedings.[7]

At its meeting on *22 May 2000*, the DSB considered a request by Canada for authorization to take appropriate countermeasures pursuant to Article 4.10 of the SCM Agreement and Article 22.2 of the DSU (WT/DS46/16).

The representatives of Canada, Brazil, European Communities, Uruguay, United States, Malaysia, India, Argentina, Saint Lucia and Hong Kong, China and the Chairman spoke.

The DSB took note of the statements and agreed that, as requested by Brazil pursuant to Article 4.11 of the SCM Agreement and Article 22.6 of the DSU, the matter be referred to arbitration to determine whether the countermeasures requested by Canada in document WT/DS46/16 were appropriate; it being understood that no countermeasures would be sought pending the Appellate Body Report and until after the Arbitration Report in the present case.

(ii) Export financing programme for aircraft – Recourse by Canada to Article 21.5 of the DSU (WT/DSB/M/87)

At its meeting on *4 August 2000*, the DSB considered the Appellate Body Report contained in WT/DS46/AB/RW and the Panel Report contained in WT/DS46/RW reconvened in accordance with Article 21.5 of the DSU to examine Brazil's implementation of the DSB's recommendations on this matter.

The representatives of Canada, Brazil and the European Communities spoke.

The DSB took note of the statements and adopted the Appellate Body Report contained in WT/DS46/AB/RW and the Panel Report contained in WT/DS46/RW as modified by the Appellate Body Report.

(d) Canada

(i) Certain measures affecting the automotive industry (WT/DSB/M/84, 86)

In February 1999,[8] the DSB had established a single panel to examine the complaints by Japan and the European Communities with regard to certain aspects

---

[7] After the meeting Australia reserved its third-party rights to participate in the Panel's proceedings.
[8] WT/DSB/M/54.

of Canada's automotive trade regime. In March 2000, Canada had notified the DSB of its decision to appeal certain issues of law and legal interpretations developed by the Panel.

At its meeting on *19 June 2000*, the DSB considered the Appellate Body Report contained in WT/DS139/AB/R–WT/DS142/AB/R and the Panel Report contained in WT/DS139/R–WT/DS142/R pertaining to the complaints by Japan and the European Communities.

The representatives of the European Communities, Japan, Canada, the Philippines and Hong Kong, China spoke.

The DSB took note of the statements and adopted the Appellate Body Report contained in WT/DS139/AB/R–WT/DS142/AB/R and the Panel Report contained in WT/DS139/R–WT/DS142/R as modified by the Appellate Body Report.

At the DSB meeting on *27 July 2000*, the representative of Canada informed the DSB of his country's intentions in respect of implementation of the DSB's recommendations on this matter, pursuant to Article 21.3 of the DSU. He said that Canada was consulting with the EC and Japan on a reasonable period of time for implementation.

The representatives of Canada, European Communities and Japan spoke.

The DSB took note of the statements and of the information provided by Canada regarding its intentions in respect of implementation of the DSB's recommendations.

(ii) Measures affecting the importation of milk and the exportation of dairy products (WT/DSB/M/70, 71, 74)

In March 1998,[9] the DSB had established a panel to examine this matter at the request of the United States. On the same date, the DSB had established a panel to examine the same matter at the request of New Zealand. Furthermore, the DSB agreed that a single panel examine both complaints. In July 1999, Canada had notified the DSB of its decision to appeal certain issues of law and legal interpretations developed by the Panel.

At its meeting on *27 October and 3 November 1999*, the DSB considered the Appellate Body Report contained in WT/DS103/AB/R–WT/DS113/AB/R and the Panel Report contained in WT/DS103/R–WT/DS113/R pertaining to the complaint by the United States and New Zealand.

The representatives of the United States, New Zealand, Canada and Australia spoke.

The DSB took note of the statements and adopted the Appellate Body Report contained in WT/DS103/AB/R–WT/DS113/AB/R and the Panel Report contained in WT/DS103/R–WT/DS113/R as modified by the Appellate Body Report.

---

[9] WT/DSB/M/44.

At its meeting on *19 November 1999*, the representative of Canada informed the DSB of his country's intentions in respect of implementation of the DSB's recommendations on this matter, pursuant to Article 21.3 of the DSU. He said that Canada would continue to consult with the United States and New Zealand on a reasonable period of time for implementation.

The representatives of Canada, United States and New Zealand spoke.

The DSB took note of the statements and of the information provided by Canada regarding its intentions in respect of implementation of the DSB's recommendations.

At the DSB meeting on *27 January 2000*, the representative of Canada informed the DSB that his country had reached an agreement with New Zealand and the United States on a reasonable period of time for implementation of the DSB's recommendations.

The representatives of Canada, New Zealand and the United States spoke.

The DSB took note of the statements.

(iii) Measures affecting the export of civilian aircraft (WT/DSB/M/71, 72)

At the DSB meeting on *19 November 1999*, the representative of Brazil made a statement concerning the implementation by Canada of the DSB's recommendations on this matter (WT/DS70).

The representatives of Brazil and Canada spoke.

The DSB took note of the statements.

At its meeting on *9 December 1999*, the DSB considered a request by Brazil under Article 21.5 of the DSU to examine Canada's implementation of the DSB's recommendations on this matter (WT/DS70/9).

The representatives of Brazil, Canada and India spoke.

The DSB took note of the statements and agreed to refer to the original Panel, pursuant to Article 21.5 of the DSU, the matter raised by Brazil in document WT/DS70/9. It was agreed that the Panel would have standard terms of reference.

The representatives of the European Communities and the United States reserved their third-party rights to participate in the Panel's proceedings.[10]

(iv) Measures affecting the export of civilian aircraft – Recourse by Brazil to Article 21.5 of the DSU (WT/DSB/M/87)

At its meeting on *4 August 2000*, the DSB considered the Appellate Body Report contained in WT/DS70/AB/RW and the Panel Report contained in WT/DS70/RW reconvened in accordance with Article 21.5 of the DSU to examine Canada's implementation with the DSB's recommendations on this matter.

---

[10] After the meeting Australia reserved its third-party rights to participate in the Panel's proceedings.

The representatives of Canada, Brazil and the European Communities spoke.

The DSB took note of the statements and adopted the Appellate Body Report in WT/DS70/AB/RW and the Panel Report in WT/DS70/RW as modified by the Appellate Body Report.

(v) Patent protection of pharmaceutical products (WT/DSB/M/78, 79, 91)

In February 1999,[11] the DSB had established a panel to examine the complaint by the European Communities and their member States with regard to certain aspects of Canada's patent laws and regulations.

At its meeting on *7 April 2000*, the DSB considered the Panel Report contained in WT/DS114/R pertaining to the complaint by the European Communities and their member States.

The representatives of Canada, European Communities, Switzerland, India and Malaysia spoke.

The DSB took note of the statements and adopted the Panel Report contained in WT/DS114/R.

At its meeting on *25 April 2000*, the representative of Canada informed the DSB of his country's intentions in respect of implementation of the DSB's recommendations, pursuant to Article 21.3 of the DSU. She said that Canada would require a reasonable period of time in order to comply with the DSB's recommendations.

The representatives of Canada and the European Communities spoke.

The DSB took note of the statements and of the information provided by Canada regarding its intentions in respect of implementation of the DSB's recommendations.

At the DSB meeting on *23 October 2000*, the representative of Canada provided information regarding his country's implementation of the DSB's recommendations on this matter.

The DSB took note of the statement.

(vi) Term of patent protection (WT/DSB/M/90, 91)

In September 1999,[12] the DSB had established a panel to examine the complaint by the United States with regard to the grant of patent terms in Canada. In June 2000, Canada had notified the DSB of its decision to appeal certain issues of law and legal interpretations developed by the Panel.

At its meeting on *12 October 2000*, the DSB considered the Appellate Body Report in WT/DS170/AB/R and the Panel Report in WT/DS170/R, pertaining to the complaint by the United States.

The representatives of Canada, United States and Argentina spoke.

---

[11] WT/DSB/M/54.
[12] WT/DSB/M/68.

The DSB took note of the statements and adopted the Appellate Body Report contained in WT/DS170/AB/R and the Panel Report contained in WT/DS170/R as upheld by the Appellate Body Report.

At the DSB meeting on *23 October 2000*, the representative of Canada informed the DSB of his country's intentions in respect of implementation of the DSB's recommendations, pursuant to Article 21.3 of the DSU. He said that Canada would require a reasonable period of time for implementation.

The representatives of Canada and the United States spoke.

The DSB took note of the statements and of the information provided by Canada regarding its intentions in respect of implementation of the DSB's recommendations.

(e) Chile

(i) Taxes on alcoholic beverages (WT/DSB/M/73, 75)

In March 1998,[13] the DSB had established a Panel to examine the complaint by the European Communities with regard to Chile's tax regime on alcoholic beverages. In September 1999, Chile had notified the DSB of its decision to appeal certain issues of law and legal interpretations developed by the Panel.

At its meeting on *12 January 2000*, the DSB considered the Appellate Body Report contained in WT/DS87/AB/R–WT/DS110/AB/R and the Panel Report contained in WT/DS87/R–WT/DS110/R pertaining to the complaint by the European Communities.

The representatives of the European Communities, Chile and the United States spoke.

The DSB took note of the statements and adopted the Appellate Body Report contained in WT/DS87/AB/R–WT/DS110/AB/R and the Panel Report contained in WT/DS87/R–WT/DS110/R as modified by the Appellate Body Report.

At the DSB meeting on *11 February 2000*, the representative of Chile informed the DSB of his country's intentions in respect of implementation of the DSB's recommendations on this matter, pursuant to Article 21.3 of the DSU. He said that Chile would need a reasonable period of time for implementation.

The representatives of Chile, European Communities and the United States spoke.

The DSB took note of the statements and of the information provided by Chile regarding its intentions in respect of implementation of the DSB's recommendations.

(ii) Measures affecting the transit and importation of swordfish (WT/DSB/M/92)

At its meeting on *17 November 2000*, the DSB considered a request by the European Communities for the establishment of a panel to examine its

---

[13] WT/DSB/M/44.

complaint with regard to Chile's measures affecting the transit and importation of swordfish (WT/DS193/2).

The representatives of the European Communities and Chile spoke.

The DSB took note of the statements and agreed to revert to this matter.

(f) Colombia

(i) Safeguard measure on imports of plain polyester filaments from Thailand (WT/DSB/M/70)

At the DSB meeting on *27 October and 3 November 1999*, Thailand sought confirmation from Colombia as to whether its safeguard measure had expired. Following Colombia's confirmation that the measure had expired and that it would not be extended, Thailand requested a withdrawal of the panel request (WT/DS181/1).

The representatives of Thailand, Colombia and the Chairman spoke.

The DSB took note of the statements and agreed that Thailand's request for a panel be withdrawn from the agenda.

(g) European Communities

(i) Anti-dumping duties on imports of cotton-type bed linen from India (WT/DSB/M/70)

At its meeting on *27 October and 3 November 1999*, the DSB considered a request by India for the establishment of a panel to examine its complaint with regard to the EC anti-dumping duties imposed on imports of cotton-type bed linen from India (WT/DS141/3).

The representatives of India and the European Communities spoke.

The DSB took note of the statements and agreed to establish a panel in accordance with the provisions of Article 6 of the DSU, with standard terms of reference.

The representatives of Egypt, Japan and the United States reserved their third-party rights to participate in the Panel's proceedings.

(ii) Regime for the importation, sale and distribution of bananas (WT/DSB/M/71, 78, 80)

At its meeting on *19 November 1999*, the DSB considered a request by Ecuador under Article 22.2 of the DSU for authorization to suspend the application to the EC and its member States of tariff concessions or other related obligations under the GATT 1994, TRIPS Agreement and the GATS (WT/DS27/52).

The representatives of Ecuador, European Communities, Honduras, Guatemala, Saint Lucia, Panama, Jamaica, Côte d'Ivoire and Malaysia spoke.

The DSB took note of the statements and agreed that the matter be referred to arbitration in accordance with Article 22.6 of the DSU.

At the DSB meeting on *7 April 2000*, the representative of Ecuador made a statement regarding his country's position on the result of the arbitration contained in WT/DS27/ARB/ECU, which had been requested by the EC in response to Ecuador's request for suspension of concessions in relation to the banana case.

The representatives of Ecuador, European Communities, Guatemala, Honduras, Saint Lucia, United States and Panama spoke.

The DSB took not of the statements.

At its meeting on *18 May 2000*, the DSB considered Ecuador's request under Article 22.7 of the DSU (WT/DS27/54) for authorization from the DSB to suspend the application to the EC and its member States of tariff concessions or other related obligations under the TRIPS Agreement, GATS and the GATT 1994.

The representatives of Ecuador and the European Communities spoke.

The DSB took note of the statements and pursuant to Ecuador's request under Article 22.7 of the DSU, as revised in the light of the Arbitrators' decision, agreed to grant authorization to suspend the application to the EC and its member States of tariff concessions or other related obligations consistent with the Arbitrators' decision contained in document WT/DS27/ARB/ECU.

(h) Guatemala

(i) Definitive anti-dumping measures on grey Portland cement from Mexico (WT/DSB/M/92)

In September 1999,[14] the DSB had established a panel to examine the complaint by Mexico with regard to Guatemala's definitive anti-dumping measures on grey Portland cement from Mexico.

At its meeting on *17 November 2000*, the DSB considered the Panel Report contained in WT/DS156/R pertaining to the complaint by Mexico.

The representatives of Mexico and Guatemala spoke.

The DSB took note of the statements and adopted the Panel Report contained in WT/DS156/R.

(i) India

(i) Measures affecting trade and investment in the motor vehicle sector (WT/DSB/M/84, 86)

At its meeting on *19 June 2000*, the DSB considered a request by the United States for the establishment of a panel to examine India's measures affecting trade and investment in the motor vehicle sector (WT/DS175/4).

---

[14] WT/DSB/M/68.

The representatives of the United States, India, Philippines and Cuba spoke.
The DSB took note of the statements and agreed to revert to this matter.
At its meeting on *27 July 2000*, the DSB again considered this matter.
The representatives of the United States, India, Malaysia, Cuba and the Philippines spoke.
The DSB took note of the statements and agreed to establish a panel in accordance with the provisions of Article 6 of the DSU, with standard terms of reference.
The representatives of the European Communities and Korea reserved their third-party rights to participate in the Panel's proceedings.[15]

(ii) Measures affecting export of certain commodities (WT/DSB/M/91)

At its meeting on *23 October 2000*, the DSB considered a request by the European Communities for the establishment of a panel to examine India's measures affecting export of certain commodities (WT/DS120/2).
The representatives of the European Communities and India spoke.
The DSB took note of the statements and agreed to revert to this matter.

(iii) Measures affecting the automotive sector (WTDSB/M/91, 92)

At its meeting on *23 October 2000*, the DSB considered a request by the European Communities for the establishment of a panel to examine India's measures affecting the automotive sector (WT/DS146/4).
The representatives of the European Communities, India, Pakistan and the Philippines spoke.
The DSB took note of the statements and agreed to revert to this matter.
At its meeting on *17 November 2000*, the DSB again considered this matter.
The representatives of the European Communities, India and the United States spoke.
The DSB took note of the statements and, in accordance with Article 9.1 of the DSU, agreed that the Panel established on 27 July 2000 to examine the complaint by the United States in document WT/DS175/4 should also examine the complaint by the European Communities in document WT/DS146/4, provided that the rights which the parties to the dispute would have enjoyed had separate panels examined the complaints are in no way impaired. It was agreed that the Panel would have standard terms of reference referring to both of the relevant documents. As the composition of the Panel in the parallel case between India and the United States was presently in the hands of the Director-General, pursuant to Article 8.7 of the DSU, it was also agreed that the EC would be included in the consultations on this matter. The Chairman recalled that Japan and Korea had reserved their third-party rights to participate in the

---

[15] After the meeting Japan reserved its third-party rights to participate in the Panel's proceedings.

Panel established to examine the complaint by the United States. Japan indicated that it wished to reserve its third-party rights to participate in the Panel established at the present meeting.

(j) Korea

(i) Definitive safeguard measure on imports of certain dairy products (WT/DSB/M/73, 75)

In July 1998,[16] the DSB had agreed to establish a Panel to examine the complaint by the European Communities with regard to a definitive safeguard measure imposed by Korea on imports of certain dairy products. In September 1999, Korea had notified the DSB of its decision to appeal certain issues of law and legal interpretations developed by the Panel.

At its meeting on *12 January 2000*, the DSB considered the Appellate Body Report contained in WT/DS98/AB/R and the Panel Report contained in WT/DS98/R and Corr.1 pertaining to the complaint by the European Communities.

The representatives of the European Communities and Korea spoke.

The DSB took note of the statements and adopted the Appellate Boy Report in WT/DS98/AB/R and the Panel Report in WT/DS98/R and Corr.1 as modified by the Appellate Body Report.

At the DSB meeting on *11 February 2000*, the representative of Korea informed the DSB of his country's intentions in respect of implementation of the DSB's recommendations on this matter, pursuant to Article 21.3 of the DSU.

The representatives of Korea, European Communities and Ecuador spoke.

The DSB took note of the statements and of the information provided by Korea regarding its intentions in respect of implementation of the DSB's recommendations.

(ii) Measures affecting government procurement (WT/DSB/M/84)

In June 1999,[17] the DSB had agreed to establish a panel to examine the complaint by the United States with regard to Korea's measures affecting government procurement.

At its meeting on *19 June 2000*, the DSB considered the Panel Report contained in WT/DS163/R pertaining to the complaint by the United States.

The representatives of Korea, United States, Philippines, India and Hong Kong, China and the Chairman spoke.

The DSB took note of the statements and adopted the Panel Report contained in WT/DS163/R; it being noted that the adoption was being

---

[16] WT/DSB/M/47.
[17] WT/DSB/M/64.

agreed only by the parties to the Plurilateral Trade Agreement at issue in this case.

(k) Mexico

(i) Anti-dumping investigation of high-fructose corn syrup (HFCS) from the United States (WT/DSB/M/76, 77, 89, 91)

In November 1998,[18] the DSB had established a panel to examine the complaint by the United States with regard to Mexico's anti-dumping investigation of high-fructose corn syrup from the United States.

At its meeting on *24 February 2000*, the DSB considered the Panel Report contained in WT/DS132/R and Corr.1 pertaining to the complaint by the United States.

The representatives of the United States, Mexico and Turkey spoke.

The DSB took note of the statements and adopted the Panel Report contained in WT/DS132/R and Corr.1.

At the DSB meeting on *20 March 2000*, the representative of Mexico informed the DSB of his country's intentions in respect of implementation of the DSB's recommendations on this matter, pursuant to Article 21.3 of the DSU. He said that his country would require a reasonable period of time in order to comply with the DSB's recommendations.

The representatives of Mexico and the United States spoke.

The DSB took note of the statements and of the information provided by Mexico regarding its intentions in respect of implementation of the DSB's recommendations.

At the DSB meeting on *26 September 2000*, the representative of the United States sought information from Mexico on the status of its implementation in this case.

The representatives of the United States and Mexico spoke.

The DSB took note of the statements.

At its meeting on *23 October 2000*, the DSB considered a request by the United States under Article 21.5 of the DSU to examine Mexico's implementation of the DSB's recommendations on this matter (WT/DS132/6).

The representatives of the United States and Mexico spoke.

The DSB took note of the statements and agreed, pursuant to Article 21.5 of the DSU, to refer to the original Panel the matter raised by the United States in document WT/DS132/6. It was agreed that the Panel would have standard terms of reference.

The representatives of the European Communities and Mauritius reserved their third-party rights to participate in the Panel's proceedings.[19]

---

[18] WT/DSB/M/51.

[19] After the meeting Jamaica reserved its third-party rights to participate in the Panel's proceedings.

(l) Nicaragua

(i) Measures affecting imports from Honduras and Colombia (WT/DSB/M/78, 80)

At its meeting on *7 April 2000*, the DSB considered a request from Colombia for the establishment of a panel to examine its complaint with regard to Nicaragua's measures affecting imports from Honduras and Colombia (WT/DS188/2 and Corr.1).

The representatives of Colombia, Nicaragua and Honduras spoke.

The DSB took note of the statements and agreed to revert to his matter.

At its meeting on *18 May 2000*, the DSB again considered this matter.

The representatives of Colombia, Nicaragua, United States, Japan, Canada, Honduras, European Communities and the Chairman spoke.

The DSB took note of the statements and agreed to establish a panel in accordance with the provisions of Article 6 of the DSU. With regard to the terms of reference, the DSB authorized the Chairman to draw up the terms of reference of the panel in consultation with the parties to the dispute subject to the provisions of Article 7.1 of the DSU.

The representatives of Canada, Costa Rica, European Communities and Honduras reserved their third-party rights to participate in the Panel's proceedings.

(m) Philippines

(i) Measures affecting trade and investment in the motor vehicle sector (WT/DSB/M/91, 92)

At its meeting on *23 October 2000*, the DSB considered a request by the United States for the establishment of a panel to examine the Philippines' measures affecting trade and investment in the motor vehicle sector (WT/DS195/3).

The representatives of the United States, Philippines, Japan, Malaysia, Argentina, Pakistan, Mexico, Indonesia and Mauritius spoke.

The DSB took note of the statements and agreed to revert to this matter.

At its meeting on *17 November 2000*, the DSB again considered this matter.

The representatives of the United States, Philippines, Thailand, India, Pakistan, Argentina, Saint Lucia, Brazil, Malaysia, Japan, Colombia, Venezuela, Chile, Singapore, Indonesia, Jamaica, Ecuador, European Communities, Hungary and Hong Kong, China and the Chairman spoke.

The DSB took note of the statements and agreed to establish a panel in accordance with the provisions of Article 6 of the DSU, with standard terms of reference.

The representatives of India and Japan reserved their third-party rights to participate in the Panel's proceedings.

(n) Thailand

(i) Anti-dumping duties on angles, shapes and sections of iron or non-alloy steel and H-beams from Poland (WT/DSB/M/70, 71)

At its meeting on *27 October and 3 November 1999*, the DSB considered a request by Poland for the establishment of a panel to examine its complaint with regard to an anti-dumping investigation initiated by Thailand concerning imports of angles, shapes and sections of iron or non-alloy steel and H-beams from Poland (WT/DS122/2).

The representatives of Poland and Thailand spoke.

The DSB took note of the statements and agreed to revert to this matter.

At its meeting on *19 November 1999*, the DSB again considered this matter.

The representatives of Poland and Thailand spoke.

The DSB took note of the statements and agreed to establish a panel in accordance with the provisions of Article 6 of the DSU, with standard terms of reference.

The representatives of the European Communities, Japan and the United States reserved their third-party rights to participate in the Panel's proceedings.

(o) Turkey

(i) Restrictions on imports of textile and clothing products (WT/DSB/M/71)

In March 1998,[20] the DSB had established a panel to examine the complaint by India with regard to Turkey's restrictions on imports of a broad range of textile and clothing products. In July 1999, Turkey had notified the DSB of its decision to appeal certain issues of law and legal interpretations developed by the Panel.

At its meeting on *19 November 1999*, the DSB considered the Appellate Body Report contained in WT/DS34/AB/R and the Panel Report contained in WT/DS34/R pertaining to the complaint by India.

The representatives of India, Turkey, Australia and Hong Kong, China spoke.

The DSB took note of the statements and adopted the Appellate Body Report contained in WT/DS34/AB/R and the Panel Report contained in WT/DS34/R as modified by the Appellate Body Report.

(p) United States

(i) Anti-Dumping Act of 1916 (WT/DSB/M/89, 91)

In February 1999,[21] the DSB had established a panel to examine the complaint by the EC with respect to the US Anti-Dumping Act of 1916. In July

---

[20] WT/DSB/M/43 and Corr.1.
[21] WT/DSB/M/54.

1999,[22] the DSB had established a panel to examine the complaint by Japan on the same matter. In May 2000, the United States had notified the DSB of its decision to appeal certain issues of law and legal interpretations developed by the Panels.

At its meeting on *26 September 2000*, the DSB considered the Appellate Body Report contained in WT/DS136/AB/R–WT/DS162/AB/R and the Panel Reports contained in WT/DS136/R and WT/DS162/R pertaining to the complaints by the EC and Japan. The Chairman drew attention to the communication from Mexico in WT/DS162/8 containing its concerns about the way in which the Panel Report pertaining to the complaint by Japan (WT/DS162/R) had been handled.

The representatives of the European Communities, Japan, United States, Mexico, India, Australia and Hong Kong, China and the Chairman spoke.

The DSB took note of the statements and adopted the Appellate Body Report contained in WT/DS136/AB/R–WT/DS162/AB/R and the Panel Reports contained in WT/DS136/R and WT/DS162/R as upheld by the Appellate Body Report.

At the DSB meeting on *23 October 2000*, the representative of the United States informed the DSB of her country's intentions in respect of implementation of the DSB's recommendations on this matter, pursuant to Article 21.3 of the DSU. She said that the United States would require a reasonable period of time for implementation.

The representatives of the United States, Japan and the European Communities spoke.

The DSB took note of the statements and of the information provided by the United States regarding its intentions in respect of implementation of the DSB's recommendations.

(ii) Anti-dumping duty on dynamic random access memory semiconductors (DRAMS) of one megabit or above from Korea (WT/DSB/M/76, 79)

At its meeting on *24 February 2000*, the representative of Korea made a statement concerning the implementation by the United States of the DSB's recommendations on this matter (WT/DS99).

The representatives of Korea and the United States spoke.

The DSB took note of the statements.

At its meeting on *25 April 2000*, the DSB considered a request from Korea under Article 21.5 of the DSU to reconvene the original Panel to examine the US implementation of the DSB's recommendations on this matter (WT/DS99/8).

The representatives of Korea and the United States spoke.

---

[22] WT/DSB/M/65.

The DSB took note of the statements and agreed to refer to the original Panel, pursuant to Article 21.5 of the DSU, the matter raised by Korea in document WT/DS99/8.

The European Communities reserved its third-party rights to participate in the Panel's proceedings.

(iii) Anti-dumping measures on certain hot-rolled steel products from Japan (WT/DSB/M/76, 77)

At its meeting on *24 February 2000*, the DSB considered a request by Japan for the establishment of a panel to examine its complaint with regard to the US anti-dumping measures on certain hot-rolled steel products from Japan (WT/DS184/2).

The representatives of Japan and the United States spoke.

The DSB took note of the statements and agreed to revert to this matter.

At its meeting on *20 March 2000*, the DSB again considered this matter.

The representatives of Japan, United States and Brazil spoke.

The DSB took note of the statements and agreed to establish a panel in accordance with the provisions of Article 6 of the DSU, with standard terms of reference.

The representatives of Canada, Chile, European Communities and Korea reserved their third-party rights to participate in the Panel's proceedings.[23]

(iv) Anti-dumping measures on stainless steel plate in coils and stainless steel sheet and strip from Korea (WT/DSB/M/70, 71, 79)

At its meeting on *27 October and 3 November 1999*, the DSB considered a request by Korea for the establishment of a panel to examine its complaint with regard to US definitive anti-dumping duties on stainless steel plate in coils and stainless steel sheet and strip from Korea (WT/DS179/2).

The representatives of Korea and the United States spoke.

The DSB took note of the statements and agreed to revert to this matter.

At its meeting on *19 November 1999*, the DSB again considered this matter.

The representatives of Korea and the United States spoke.

The DSB took note of the statements and agreed to establish a panel in accordance with the provisions of Article 6 of the DSU, with standard terms of reference.

The representatives of the European Communities and Japan reserved their third-party rights to participate in the Panel's proceedings.

---

[23] After the meeting Brazil reserved its third-party rights to participate in the Panel's proceedings.

(v) Definitive safeguard measures on imports of circular welded carbon quality line pipe from Korea (WT/DSB/M/89, 91)

At its meeting on *26 September 2000*, the DSB considered a request by Korea for the establishment of a panel to examine US definitive safeguard measures on imports of circular welded carbon quality line pipe from Korea (WT/DS202/4).

The representatives of Korea and the United States spoke.

The DSB took note of the statements and agreed to revert to this matter.

At its meeting on *23 October 2000*, the DSB again considered this matter.

The representatives of Korea, United States and the European Communities spoke.

The DSB took note of the statements and agreed to establish a panel in accordance with the provisions of Article 6 of the DSU, with standard terms of reference.

The representatives of the European Communities, Canada, Japan and Mexico reserved their third-party rights to participate in the Panel's proceedings.[24]

(vi) Import prohibition of certain shrimp and shrimp products (WT/DSB/M/91)

At its meeting on *23 October 2000*, the DSB considered a request by Malaysia under Article 21.5 of the DSU to examine the US implementation of the DSB's recommendations on this matter (WT/DS58/17).

The representatives of Malaysia, United States, Thailand, India and Australia spoke.

The DSB took note of the statements and agreed, pursuant to Article 21.5 of the DSU, to refer to the original Panel the matter raised by Malaysia in document WT/DS58/17. It was agreed that the Panel would have standard terms of reference.

The representatives of Canada, Ecuador, India, Japan, Mexico, Thailand and Hong Kong, China reserved their third-party rights to participate in the Panel's proceedings.[25]

(vii) Imposition of countervailing duties on certain hot-rolled lead and bismuth carbon steel products originating in the United Kingdom (WT/DSB/M/83, 85 and Corr.1)

In February 1999,[26] the DSB had established a panel to examine the complaint by the EC with regard to the US countervailing duties on certain hot-rolled lead and bismuth carbon steel products originating in the United Kingdom. In

---

[24] After the meeting Australia reserved its third-party rights to participate in the Panel's proceedings.

[25] After the meeting Australia, European Communities and Pakistan reserved their third-party rights to participate in the Panel's proceedings.

[26] WT/DSB/M/55 and Corr.1.

January 2000, the EC had notified the DSB of its decision to appeal certain issues of law and legal interpretations developed by the Panel.

At its meeting on *7 June 2000*, the DSB considered the Appellate Body Report contained in WT/DS138/AB/R and the Panel Report contained in WT/DS138/R pertaining to the complaint by the European Communities.

The representatives of the European Communities, United States, Mexico, Canada, Japan, Argentina, Hungary, India, Philippines, Brazil, Malaysia, Pakistan, Ecuador, Australia, Thailand and Hong Kong, China and the Chairman spoke.

The DSB took note of the statements and adopted the Appellate Body Report contained in WT/DS138/AB/R and the Panel Report contained in WT/DS138/R as upheld by the Appellate Body Report.

At the DSB meeting on *5 July 2000*, the representative of the United States informed the DSB of her country's implementation of the DSB's recommendations in this case.

The representatives of the United States, European Communities and Brazil spoke.

The DSB took note of the statements and of the information provided by the United States with respect of implementation of the DSB's recommendations.

(viii) Measures treating export restraints as subsidies (WT/DSB/M/87, 88)

At its meeting on *4 August 2000*, the DSB considered a request by Canada for the establishment of a panel to examine its complaint with regard to the United States' measures treating an export restraint of a product as a subsidy to producers of other products made, using or incorporating the restricted product if the domestic price of that product was affected by the restraint (WT/DS194/2).

The representatives of Canada and the United States spoke.

The DSB took note of the statements and agreed to revert to this matter.

At its meeting on *11 September 2000*, the DSB again considered this matter.

The representatives of Canada and the United States spoke.

The DSB took note of the statements and agreed to establish a panel in accordance with the provisions of Article 6 of the DSU, with standard terms of reference.

The representatives of Australia, European Communities and India reserved their third-party rights to participate in the Panel's proceedings.

(ix) Safeguard measure on imports of lamb meat from New Zealand and Australia (WT/DSB/M/70, 71)

At its meeting on *27 October and 3 November 1999*, the DSB considered a request by New Zealand (WT/DS177/4) and Australia (WT/DS178/5) to examine their complaints with regard to safeguard measures imposed by the United States on imports of lamb meat.

The representatives of New Zealand, Australia, United States and the Chairman spoke.

The DSB took note of the statements and agreed to revert to this matter.

At its meeting on *19 November 1999*, the DSB again considered this matter.

The representatives of New Zealand, Australia and the United States spoke.

The DSB took note of the statements and agreed to establish a single panel pursuant to Article 9 of the DSU, with standard terms of reference.

The representatives of Canada, European Communities, Iceland, and Japan reserved their third-party rights to participate in the Panel's proceedings. Australia reserved its third-party rights in respect of New Zealand's complaint. New Zealand reserved its third-party rights in respect of Australia's complaint.

(x) Section 110(5) of the US Copyright Act (WT/DSB/M/86, 88)

In May 1999,[27] the DSB had established a panel to examine the complaint by the EC with regard to Section 110(5) of the US Copyright Act.

At its meeting on *27 July 2000*, the DSB considered the Panel Report contained in WT/DS160/R pertaining to the complaint by the European Communities.

The representatives of the European Communities, United States, Philippines, Australia, Switzerland, India, Mexico, Malaysia and Hong Kong, China and the Chairman spoke.

The DSB took note of the statements and adopted the Panel Report contained in WT/DS160/R.

At the DSB meeting on *11 September 2000*, the representative of the United States informed the DSB of her country's intentions with regard to implementation of the DSB's recommendations on this matter. She said that the United States would need a reasonable period of time for implementation.

The representatives of the United States, European Communities and Australia spoke.

The DSB took note of the statements and of the information provided by the United States regarding its intentions in respect of implementation of the DSB's recommendations. The DSB also noted that the question of a reasonable period of time would be a matter for further consideration by the parties under Article 21.3(b) of the DSU.

(xi) Section 211 Omnibus Appropriations Act of 1998 (WT/DSB/M/86, 89)

At its meeting on *27 July 2000*, the DSB considered a request by the European Communities and their member States for the establishment of a panel to

---

[27] WT/DSB/M/62.

examine their complaint in relation to US Section 211 Omnibus Appropriations Act of 1998 (WT/DS176/2).

The representatives of the European Communities, United States and Cuba spoke.

The DSB took note of the statements and agreed to revert to this matter.

At its meeting on *26 September 2000*, the DSB again considered this matter.

The representatives of the European Communities, United States and Cuba spoke.

The DSB took note of the statements and agreed to establish a panel in accordance with Article 6 of the DSU, with standard terms of reference.

The representatives of Japan and Nicaragua reserved their third-party rights to participate in the Panel's proceedings.[28]

(xii) Sections 301–310 of the Trade Act of 1974 (WT/DSB/M/74)

In March 1999,[29] the DSB had established a panel to examine the complaint by the European Communities with regard to Section 301–310 of the US Trade Act of 1974.

At its meeting on *27 January 2000*, the DSB considered the Panel Report contained in WT/DS152/R pertaining to the complaint by the European Communities.

The representatives of the United States, European Communities, Japan, Brazil, Korea, Costa Rica, Cuba, Thailand, Saint Lucia, Norway, Canada, Poland (on behalf of CEFTA Members and Estonia and Latvia), Dominican Republic, Jamaica, India, Australia, Argentina, Egypt, Guatemala and Hong Kong, China spoke.

The DSB took note of the statements and adopted the Panel Report contained in WT/DS152/R.

(xiii) Tax treatment for 'Foreign Sales Corporations' (WT/DSB/M/77, 78, 90, 92)

In September 1998,[30] the DSB had established a panel to examine the complaint by the European Communities with regard to US tax treatment for 'Foreign Sales Corporations'. In November 1999, the United States had notified the DSB of its decision to appeal certain issues of law and legal interpretations developed by the Panel.

At its meeting on *20 March 2000*, the DSB considered the Appellate Body Report contained in WT/DS108/AB/R and the Panel Report contained in WT/DS108/R pertaining to the complaint by the European Communities.

The representatives of the European Communities, United States, Canada and Australia spoke.

---

[28] After the meeting Canada reserved its third-party rights to participate in the Panel's proceedings.
[29] WT/DSB/M/56.
[30] WT/DSB/M/48.

The DSB took note of the statements and adopted the Appellate Body Report in WT/DS108/AB/R and the Panel Report in WT/DS108/R as modified by the Appellate Body Report.

At the DSB meeting on *7 April 2000*, the representative of the United States informed the DSB of her country's intentions in respect of implementation of the DSB's recommendations on this matter.

The representatives of the United States and the European Communities spoke.

The DSB took note of the statements and of the information provided by the United States regarding its intentions in respect of implementation of the DSB's recommendations.

At the DSB meeting on *12 October 2000*, the representative of the United States requested the DSB to modify the time-period for compliance (1 October 2000) in the FSC dispute so as to expire on 1 November 2000.

The representatives of the United States, European Communities, Japan and the Chairman spoke.

The DSB took note of the statements and, given that there was no opposition to the US request, acceded to the request of the United States, as formulated in its letter of 29 September 2000 and circulated in document WT/DS108/11.

At the DSB meeting on *17 November 2000*, the United States announced that on 15 November 2000, the US President had signed into law H.R. 4986, the FSC Repeal and Extraterritorial Income Exclusion Act of 2000. The United States considered that with the enactment of this legislation, it had implemented the DSB's recommendations in the FSC case. The EC stated that the new legislation did not bring the United States into compliance with the DSB's recommendations and that it would enter into Article 21.5 consultations with the United States on this matter. In order to protect its rights, the EC requested a special meeting of the DSB on 28 November 2000 to seek authorization to take appropriate countermeasures and to suspend concessions in accordance with Article 4.10 of the SCM Agreement and Article 22.2 of the DSU.

The representatives of the United States and the European Communities spoke.

The DSB took note of the statements.

(xiv) Transitional safeguard measure on combed cotton yarn from Pakistan (WT/DSB/M/80, 84)

At its meeting on *18 May 2000*, the DSB considered a request by Pakistan for the establishment of a panel to examine the US transitional safeguard measure on combed cotton yarn from Pakistan (WT/DS192/1).

The representatives of Pakistan and the United States spoke.

The DSB took note of the statements and agreed to revert to this matter.

At its meeting on *19 June 2000*, the DSB again considered this matter.

The representatives of Pakistan and the United States spoke.

The DSB took note of the statements and agreed to establish a panel in accordance with the provisions of Article 6 of the DSU, with standard terms of reference.

The representatives of the European Communities and India reserved their third-party rights to participate in the Panel's proceedings.

10. Surveillance of implementation of recommendations adopted by the DSB

Matters considered by the DSB under this item are included on the agenda pursuant to Article 21.6 of the DSU which provides that: 'Unless the DSB decides otherwise, the issue of implementation of the recommendations or rulings shall be placed on the agenda of the DSB meeting after six months following the date of establishment of the reasonable time-period pursuant to paragraph 3 and shall remain on the DSB's agenda until the issue is resolved. At least 10 days prior to each such DSB meeting, the Member concerned shall provide the DSB with a status report in writing of its progress in the implementation of the recommendations or rulings.'

(a) Canada

(i) Measures affecting the importation of milk and the exportation of dairy products (WT/DSBM/84, 86, 89, 91, 92)

At its meeting on *19 June 2000*, the DSB considered the status report by Canada on its progress in the implementation of the DSB's recommendations on this matter (WT/DS103/12–WT/DS113/12).

The representatives of Canada, United States and New Zealand spoke.

The DSB took note of the statements and agreed to revert to this matter at its next regular meeting.

At its meeting on *27 July 2000*, the DSB considered the status report by Canada on its progress in the implementation of the DSB's recommendations on this matter (WT/DS103/12/Add.1–WT/DS113/12/Add.1).

The representatives of Canada, New Zealand and the United States spoke.

The DSB took note of the statements and agreed to revert to this matter at its next regular meeting.

At its meeting on *26 September 2000*, the DSB considered the status report by Canada on its progress in the implementation of the DSB's recommendations on this matter (WT/DS103/12/Add.2–WT/DS113/12/Add.2).

The representatives of Canada, New Zealand and the United States spoke.

The DSB took note of the statements and agreed to revert to this matter at its next regular meeting.

At its meeting on *23 October 2000*, the DSB considered the status report by Canada on its progress in the implementation of the DSB's recommendations on this matter (WT/DS103/12/Add.3–WT/DS113/12/Add.3).

The representatives of Canada, New Zealand and the United States spoke.

The DSB took note of the statements and agreed to revert to this matter at its next regular meeting.

At its meeting on *17 November 2000*, the DSB considered the status report by Canada on its progress in the implementation of the DSB's recommendations on this matter (WT/DS103/12/Add.4–WT/DS113/12/Add.4).

The representatives of Canada, New Zealand and the United States spoke.

The DSB took note of the statements and agreed to revert to this matter at its next regular meeting.

(b) European Communities

(i) Regime for the importation, sale and distribution of bananas (WT/DSB/M/70, 71, 74, 76, 77, 78, 80, 84, 86, 89, 91, 92)

At the its meeting on *27 October and 3 November 1999*, the DSB considered the status report by the EC contained in WT/DS27/51/Add.2.

The representatives of the European Communities, Ecuador, United States, Mexico, Honduras, Guatemala, Colombia and Panama spoke.

The DSB took note of the statements and agreed to revert to this matter at its next regular meeting.

At its meeting on *19 November 1999*, the DSB considered the status report by the EC on its progress in the implementation of the DSB's recommendations on this matter (WT/DS27/51/Add.3).

The representatives of the European Communities, United States, Guatemala, Honduras, Colombia, Panama, Ecuador, Costa Rica, Mexico, Jamaica, Saint Lucia and Colombia spoke.

The DSB took note of the statements and agreed to revert to this matter at its next regular meeting.

At its meeting on *27 January 2000*, the DSB considered the status report by the EC on its progress in the implementation of the DSB's recommendations on this matter (WT/DS27/51/Add.4).

The representatives of the European Communities, Costa Rica, Guatemala, Ecuador, Panama, Honduras, Mexico and the United States spoke.

The DSB took note of the statements and agreed to revert to this matter at its next regular meeting.

At its meeting on *24 February 2000*, the DSB considered the status report by the EC on its progress in the implementation of the DSB's recommendations on this matter (WT/DS27/51/Add.5).

The representatives of the European Communities, Colombia, Guatemala, Honduras, Ecuador, Panama, Costa Rica, United States and Mexico spoke.

The DSB took note of the statements and agreed to revert to this matter at its next regular meeting.

At its meeting on *20 March 2000*, the DSB considered the status report by the EC on its progress in the implementation of the DSB's recommendations on this matter (WT/DS27/51/Add.6).

The representatives of the European Communities, Panama, Guatemala, Honduras, Saint Lucia (on behalf of Dominica and Saint Vincent and the Grenadines), United States and Ecuador spoke.

The DSB took note of the statements and agreed to revert to this matter at its next regular meeting.

At its meeting on *7 April 2000*, the DSB considered the status report by the EC on its progress in the implementation of the DSB's recommendations on this matter (WT/DS27/51/Add.7).

The representatives of the European Communities, Ecuador, Panama, Guatemala, Honduras, United States, Mexico and Saint Lucia spoke.

The DSB took note of the statements and agreed to revert to this matter at its next regular meeting.

At its meeting on *18 May 2000*, the DSB considered the status report by the EC on its progress in the implementation of the DSB's recommendations on this matter (WT/DS27/15/Add.8).

The representatives of the European Communities, Ecuador, Panama, Honduras, United States, Colombia, Guatemala, Mexico and Saint Luciaspoke.

The DSB took note of the statements and agreed to revert to this matter at its next regular meeting.

At its meeting on *19 June 2000*, the DSB considered the status report by the EC on its progress in the implementation of the DSB's recommendations on this matter (WT/DS27/51/Add.9).

The representatives of the European Communities, Ecuador, Panama, Honduras, Guatemala, United States, Saint Lucia and Mexico spoke.

The DSB took note of the statements and agreed to revert to this matter at its next regular meeting.

At its meeting on *27 July 2000*, the DSB considered the status report by the EC on its progress in the implementation of the DSB's recommendations on this matter (WT/DS27/51/Add.10).

The representatives of the European Communities, Ecuador, Honduras, Guatemala, Jamaica, Mexico, Panama, Saint Lucia, United States and Colombia spoke.

The DSB took note of the statements and agreed to revert to this matter at its next regular meeting.

At its meeting on *26 September 2000*, the DSB considered the status report by the EC on its progress in the implementation of the DSB's recommendations on this matter (WT/DS27/51/Add.11).

The representatives of the European Communities, Ecuador, Honduras, Guatemala, Panama, United States, Mexico and Saint Lucia spoke.

The DSB took note of the statements and agreed to revert to this matter at its next regular meeting.

At its meeting on the *23 October 2000*, the DSB considered the status report by the EC on its progress in the implementation of the DSB's recommendations on this matter (WT/DS27/51/Add.12).

The representatives of the European Communities, Honduras, Panama, Ecuador, Jamaica, Costa Rica, United States, Guatemala, Mexico, Dominica, Colombia, Saint Lucia, Mauritius and Suriname spoke.

The DSB took note of the statements and agreed to revert to this matter at its next regular meeting.

At its meeting on *17 November 2000*, the DSB considered the status report by the EC on its progress in the implementation of the DSB's recommendations on this matter (WT/DS27/51/Add.13).

The representatives of the European Communities, Ecuador, Colombia, Honduras, Guatemala, Panama, Mexico, United States, Nicaragua and Saint Lucia spoke.

The DSB took note of the statement and agreed to revert to this matter at its next regular meeting.

(c) India

(i) Quantitative restrictions on imports of agricultural, textile and industrial products (WT/DSB/M/86, 89, 91, 92)

At its meeting on *27 July 2000*, the DSB considered the status report by India on its progress in the implementation of the DSB's recommendations on this matter (WT/DS90/16).

The representatives of India and the United States spoke.

The DSB took note of the statements and agreed to revert to this matter at its next regular meeting.

At its meeting on *26 September 2000*, the DSB considered the status report by India on its progress in the implementation of the DSB's recommendations on this matter (WT/DS90/16/Add.1).

The representatives of India and the United States spoke.

The DSB took note of the statements and agreed to revert to this matter at its next regular meeting.

At its meeting on *23 October 2000*, the DSB considered the status report by India on its progress in the implementation of the DSB's recommendations on this matter (WT/DS90/16/Add.2).

The representatives of India and the United States spoke.

The DSB took note of the statements and agreed to revert to this matter at its next regular meeting.

At its meeting on *17 November 2000*, the DSB considered the status report by India on its progress in the implementation of the DSB's recommendations on this matter (WT/DS90/16/Add.3).

The representatives of India and the United States spoke.

The DSB took note of the statements and agreed to revert to this matter at its next regular meeting.

(d) Japan

(i) Measures affecting agricultural products (WT/DSB/M/74, 76, 77, 78, 80, 84, 86, 89, 91, 92)

At its DSB meeting on *27 January 2000*, the DSB considered the status report by Japan on its progress in the implementation of the DSB's recommendations on this matter (WT/DS76/11).

The representatives of Japan, United States, Hungary, Australia and Brazil spoke.

The DSB took note of the statements and agreed to revert to this matter at its next regular meeting.

At its meeting on *24 February 2000*, the DSB considered the status report by Japan on its progress in the implementation of the DSB's recommendations on this matter (WT/DS76/11/Add.1).

The representatives of Japan, United States and Australia spoke.

The DSB took note of the statements and agreed to revert to this matter at its next regular meeting.

At its meeting on *20 March 2000*, the DSB considered the status report by Japan on its progress in the implementation of the DSB's recommendations on this matter (WT/DS76/11/Add.2).

The representatives of Japan, United States and Australia spoke.

The DSB took note of the statements and agreed to revert to this matter at its next regular meeting.

At its meeting on *7 April 2000*, the DSB considered the status report by Japan on its progress in the implementation of the DSB's recommendations on this matter (WT/DS76/11/Add.3).

The representatives of Japan, United States and Brazil spoke.

The DSB took note of the statements and agreed to revert to this matter at its next regular meeting.

At its meeting on *18 May 2000*, the DSB considered the status report by Japan on its progress in the implementation of the DSB's recommendations on this matter (WT/DS76/11/Add.4).

The representatives of Japan and the United States spoke.

The DSB took note of the statements and agreed to revert to this matter at its next regular meeting.

At its meeting on *19 June 2000*, the DSB considered the status report by Japan on its progress in the implementation of the DSB's recommendations on this matter (WT/DS76/11/Add.5).

The representatives of Japan and the United States spoke.

The DSB took note of the statements and agreed to revert to this matter at its next regular meeting.

At its meeting on *27 July 2000*, the DSB considered the status report by Japan on its progress in the implementation of the DSB's recommendations on this matter (WT/DS76/11/Add.6).

The representatives of Japan and the United States spoke.

The DSB took note of the statements and agreed to revert to this matter at its next regular meeting.

At its meeting on *26 September 2000*, the DSB considered the status report by Japan on its progress in the implementation of the DSB's recommendations on this matter WT/DS76/11/Add.7).

The representatives of Japan, United States, European Communities and Australia spoke.

The DSB took note of the statements and agreed to revert to this matter at its next regular meeting.

At its meeting on *23 October 2000*, the DSB considered the status report by Japan on its progress in the implementation of the DSB's recommendations on this matter (WT/DS76/11/Add.8).

The representatives of Japan, United States, European Communities and Australia spoke.

The DSB took note of the statements and agreed to revert to this matter at its next regular meeting.

At its meeting on *17 November 2000*, the DSB considered the status report by Japan on its progress in the implementation of the DSB's recommendations on this matter (WT/DS76/11/Add.9).

The representatives of Japan, United States, European Communities and Hungary spoke.

The DSB took note of the statements and agreed to revert to this matter at its next regular meeting.

(e) Korea

(i) Definitive safeguard measure on imports of certain dairy products (WT/DSBM/89)

At its meeting on *26 September 2000*, the DSB considered the status report by Korea on its progress in the implementation of the DSB's recommendations on this matter (WT/DS98/12).

The representatives of Korea and the European Communities spoke.

The DSB took note of the statements.

(ii) Taxes on alcoholic beverages (WT/DSB/M/74)

At its meeting on *27 January 2000*, the DSB considered the status report by Korea on its progress in the implementation of the DSB's recommendations on this matter (WT/DS75/18–WT/DS84/16).

The representatives of Korea, European Communities and Mexico spoke.
The DSB took note of the statements.

(f) Turkey

(i) Restrictions on imports of textile and clothing products (WT/DSB/M/86, 89, 91, 92)

At its meeting on *27 July 2000*, the DSB considered the status report by Turkey on its progress in the implementation of the DSB's recommendations on this matter (WT/DS34/12).

The representatives of Turkey, India and Australia spoke.

The DSB took note of the statements and agreed to revert to this matter at its next regular meeting.

At its meeting on *26 September 2000*, the DSB considered the status report by Turkey on its progress in the implementation of the DSB's recommendations on this matter (WT/DS34/12/Add.1).

The representatives of Turkey and India spoke.

The DSB took note of the statements and agreed to revert to this matter at its next regular meeting.

At its meeting on *23 October 2000*, the DSB considered the status report by Turkey on its progress in the implementation of the DSB's recommendations on this matter (WT/DS34/12/Add.2).

The representatives of Turkey and India spoke.

The DSB took note of the statements and agreed to revert to this matter at its next regular meeting.

At its meeting on *17 November 2000*, the DSB considered the status report by Turkey on its progress in the implementation of the DSB's recommendations on this matter (WT/DS34/12/Add.3).

The representatives of Turkey and India spoke.

The DSB took note of the statements and agreed to revert to this matter at its next regular meeting.

(g) United States

(i) Anti-dumping duty on dynamic random access memory semiconductors (DRAMS) of one megabit or above from Korea (WT/DSB/M/74)

At its meeting on *27 January 2000*, the DSB considered the status report by the United States on its progress in the implementation of the DSB's recommendations on this matter (WT/DS99/6).

The representatives of the United States and Korea spoke.

The DSB took note of the statements.

(ii) Import prohibition of certain shrimp and shrimp products (WT/DSB/M/70, 71, 74)

At its meeting on *27 October and 3 November 1999*, the DSB considered the status report by the United States on its progress in the implementation of the DSB's recommendations on this matter (WT/DS58/15/Add.2).

The representatives of the United States, Malaysia, Thailand, India and Australia spoke.

The DSB took note of the statements and agreed to revert to this matter at its next regular meeting.

At its meeting on *19 November 1999*, the DSB considered the status report by the United States on its progress in the implementation of the DSB's recommendations on this matter (WT/DS58/15/Add.3).

The representatives of the United States, Malaysia, Australia, India, European Communities and Ecuador spoke.

The DSB took note of the statements and agreed to revert to this matter at its next regular meeting.

At its meeting on *27 January 2000*, the DSB considered the status report by the United States on its progress in the implementation of the DSB's recommendations on this matter (WT/DS58/15/Add.4).

The representatives of the United States, Malaysia, India, European Communities and Australia spoke.

The DSB took note of the statements.

11. Other matters

(a) United States – Measures affecting textiles and apparel products (WT/DSB/M/70)

At the DSB meeting on *27 October and 3 November 1999*, the representative of India expressed concern about the lack of notification with regard to a settlement reached by the US and the EC in relation to the dispute on US measures affecting textiles and apparel products (WT/DS151).

The representatives of India, United States, European Communities, Dominican Republic, Honduras and Hong Kong, China spoke.

The DSB took note of the statements.

(b) Indonesia – Certain measures affecting the automobile industry (WT/DSB/M/71, 77)

At the DSB meeting on *19 November 1999*, the representative of the EC made a statement concerning Indonesia's implementation of the DSB's recommendations in this case (WT/DS54).

The DSB took note of the statement.

At the DSB meeting on *20 March 2000*, the representative of the EC made a statement concerning Indonesia's implementation of the DSB's recommendations in this case.

The representatives of the European Communities and Indonesia spoke.

The DSB took note of the statements.

(c) Withdrawal of an appeal under Rule 30 of the Working Procedures for Appellate Review (WT/DSB/M/72)

At the DSB meeting on *9 December 1999*, the representative of India expressed concern about the US withdrawal of its appeal pursuant to Rule 30 of the Working Procedures for Appellate Review in the case on United States – Tax treatment for 'Foreign Sales Corporations' (WT/DS108).

The representatives of India and the United States spoke.

The DSB took note of the statements.

(d) Questions addressed by delegations to the Chairman of the DSB upon the adoption of the Reports of the Appellate Body and the Panel on 'United States – Imposition of Countervailing Duties on Certain Hot-Rolled Lead and Bismuth Carbon Steel Products Originating in the United Kingdom' at the DSB meeting on 7 June 2000 (WT/DSB/M/84)

At the DSB meeting on *19 June 2000*, the Chairman made a statement regarding this matter. The statement was subsequently circulated in document WT/DSB/W/137.

The DSB took note of the statement.

(e) Third-party participation in GATT Article XXII consultations in relation to the case on 'United States – Section 306 of the Trade Act of 1974 and Amendments Thereto' (WT/DSB/M/86)

At the DSB meeting on *27 July 2000*, the representative of Japan raised some systemic concerns regarding the US refusal of his country's request, under Article 4.11 of the DSU, to be joined in GATT Article XXII consultations requested by the EC on US Section 306 of the Trade Act of 1974 and amendments thereto (WT/DS200/1).

The representatives of Japan, Saint Lucia, Australia, Jamaica, European Communities, Ecuador, United States, Philippines and Hong Kong, China and the Chairman spoke.

The DSB took note of the statements.

(f) Information provided by the EC with regard to the agreed procedures in the follow-up to the Foreign Sales Corporations (FSC) dispute (WT/DSB/M/90)

At the DSB meeting on *12 October 2000*, the representative of the EC provided information regarding the understanding reached by the EC and the United States on the procedures in the follow-up to the FSC dispute (WT/DS108/12).

The representatives of the European Communities, India and Japan spoke.

The DSB took note of the statements.

(g) Special meeting of the General Council on 22 November 2000 to discuss the communication from the Appellate Body to the Chairman of the DSB on 'European Communities – Measures Affecting Asbestos and Asbestos – Containing Products' (WT/DSB/M/92)

At the DSB meeting on *17 November 2000*, the Chairman put forward a few personal reflections to enable delegations to prepare for the special meeting of the General Council convened in order to discuss the communication from the Appellate Body contained in WT/DS135/9.

The representatives of Canada, Brazil, Zimbabwe, India, Saint Lucia, Australia, United States, European Communities, the Chairman of the General Council and the DSB Chairman spoke.

The DSB took note of the statements.

(h) Consultations requested by Brazil with the European Communities on its measures affecting soluble coffee (WT/DSB/M/92)

At the DSB meeting on *17 November 2000*, Colombia, speaking on behalf of the Andean Community and the Central American countries, expressed concern that Brazil had requested consultations with the EC on its measures affecting soluble coffee (WT/DS209/1) pursuant to Article XXIII of GATT 1994, thereby preventing other countries having an interest in this matter to be joined in those consultations.

The representatives of Colombia, Brazil and Saint Lucia spoke.

The DSB took note of the statements.

Annex II
Understanding on Rules and Procedures Governing the Settlement of Disputes

Members hereby *agree* as follows:

Article 1
Coverage and application

1. The rules and procedures of this Understanding shall apply to disputes brought pursuant to the consultation and dispute settlement provisions of the agreements listed in Appendix 1 to this Understanding (referred to in this Understanding as the 'covered agreements'). The rules and procedures of this Understanding shall also apply to consultations and the settlement of disputes between Members concerning their rights and obligations under the provisions of the Agreement Establishing the World Trade Organization (referred to in this Understanding as the 'WTO Agreement') and of this Understanding taken in isolation or in combination with any other covered agreement.

2. The rules and procedures of this Understanding shall apply subject to such special or additional rules and procedures on dispute settlement contained in the covered agreements as are identified in Appendix 2 to this Understanding. To the extent that there is a difference between the rules and procedures of this Understanding and the special or additional rules and procedures set forth in Appendix 2, the special or additional rules and procedures in Appendix 2 shall prevail. In disputes involving rules and procedures under more than one covered agreement, if there is a conflict between special or additional rules and procedures of such agreements under review, and where the parties to the dispute cannot agree on rules and procedures within 20 days of the establishment of the panel, the Chairman of the Dispute Settlement Body provided for in paragraph 1 of Article 2 (referred to in this Understanding as the 'DSB'), in consultation with the parties to the dispute, shall determine the rules and procedures to be followed within 10 days after a request by either Member. The Chairman shall be guided by the principle that special or additional rules and procedures should be used where possible, and the rules and procedures set out in this Understanding should be used to the extent necessary to avoid conflict.

Article 2
Administration

1. The Dispute Settlement Body is hereby established to administer these rules and procedures and, except as otherwise provided in a covered agreement, the consultation and dispute settlement provisions of the covered agreements. Accordingly, the DSB shall have the authority to establish panels, adopt panel and Appellate Body reports, maintain surveillance of implementation of rulings and recommendations, and authorize suspension of concessions and other obligations under the covered agreements. With respect to disputes arising under a covered agreement which is a Plurilateral Trade Agreement, the term 'Member' as used herein shall refer only to those Members that are parties to the relevant Plurilateral Trade Agreement. Where the DSB administers the dispute settlement provisions of a Plurilateral Trade Agreement, only those Members that are parties to that Agreement may participate in decisions or actions taken by the DSB with respect to that dispute.

2. The DSB shall inform the relevant WTO Councils and Committees of any developments in disputes related to provisions of the respective covered agreements.

3. The DSB shall meet as often as necessary to carry out its functions within the time-frames provided in this Understanding.

4. Where the rules and procedures of this Understanding provide for the DSB to take a decision, it shall do so by consensus.[1]

Article 3
General provisions

1. Members affirm their adherence to the principles for the management of disputes heretofore applied under Articles XXII and XXIII of GATT 1947, and the rules and procedures as further elaborated and modified herein.

2. The dispute settlement system of the WTO is a central element in providing security and predictability to the multilateral trading system. The Members recognize that it serves to preserve the rights and obligations of Members under the covered agreements, and to clarify the existing provisions of those agreements in accordance with customary rules of interpretation of public international law. Recommendations and rulings of the DSB cannot add to or diminish the rights and obligations provided in the covered agreements.

---

[1] The DSB shall be deemed to have decided by consensus on a matter submitted for its consideration, if no Member, present at the meeting of the DSB when the decision is taken, formally objects to the proposed decision.

3. The prompt settlement of situations in which a Member considers that any benefits accruing to it directly or indirectly under the covered agreements are being impaired by measures taken by another Member is essential to the effective functioning of the WTO and the maintenance of a proper balance between the rights and obligations of Members.

4. Recommendations or rulings made by the DSB shall be aimed at achieving a satisfactory settlement of the matter in accordance with the rights and obligations under this Understanding and under the covered agreements.

5. All solutions to matters formally raised under the consultation and dispute settlement provisions of the covered agreements, including arbitration awards, shall be consistent with those agreements and shall not nullify or impair benefits accruing to any Member under those agreements, nor impede the attainment of any objective of those agreements.

6. Mutually agreed solutions to matters formally raised under the consultation and dispute settlement provisions of the covered agreements shall be notified to the DSB and the relevant Councils and Committees, where any Member may raise any point relating thereto.

7. Before bringing a case, a Member shall exercise its judgement as to whether action under these procedures would be fruitful. The aim of the dispute settlement mechanism is to secure a positive solution to a dispute. A solution mutually acceptable to the parties to a dispute and consistent with the covered agreements is clearly to be preferred. In the absence of a mutually agreed solution, the first objective of the dispute settlement mechanism is usually to secure the withdrawal of the measures concerned if these are found to be inconsistent with the provisions of any of the covered agreements. The provision of compensation should be resorted to only if the immediate withdrawal of the measure is impracticable and as a temporary measure pending the withdrawal of the measure which is inconsistent with a covered agreement. The last resort which this Understanding provides to the Member invoking the dispute settlement procedures is the possibility of suspending the application of concessions or other obligations under the covered agreements on a discriminatory basis vis-à-vis the other Member, subject to authorization by the DSB of such measures.

8. In cases where there is an infringement of the obligations assumed under a covered agreement, the action is considered *prima facie* to constitute a case of nullification or impairment. This means that there is normally a presumption that a breach of the rules has an adverse impact on other Members parties to that covered agreement, and in such cases, it shall be up to the Member against whom the complaint has been brought to rebut the charge.

9. The provisions of this Understanding are without prejudice to the rights of Members to seek authoritative interpretation of provisions of a covered agreement through decision-making under the WTO Agreement or a covered agreement which is a Plurilateral Trade Agreement.

10. It is understood that requests for conciliation and the use of the dispute settlement procedures should not be intended or considered as contentious acts

and that, if a dispute arises, all Members will engage in these procedures in good faith in an effort to resolve the dispute. It is also understood that complaints and counter-complaints in regard to distinct matters should not be linked.

11. This Understanding shall be applied only with respect to new requests for consultations under the consultation provisions of the covered agreements made on or after the date of entry into force of the WTO Agreement. With respect to disputes for which the request for consultations was made under GATT 1947 or under any other predecessor agreement to the covered agreements before the date of entry into force of the WTO Agreement, the relevant dispute settlement rules and procedures in effect immediately prior to the date of entry into force of the WTO Agreement shall continue to apply.[2]

12. Notwithstanding paragraph 11, if a complaint based on any of the covered agreements is brought by a developing country Member against a developed country Member, the complaining party shall have the right to invoke, as an alternative to the provisions contained in Articles 4, 5, 6 and 12 of this Understanding, the corresponding provisions of the Decision of 5 April 1966 (BISD 14S/18), except that where the Panel considers that the time-frame provided for in paragraph 7 of that Decision is insufficient to provide its report and with the agreement of the complaining party, that time-frame may be extended. To the extent that there is a difference between the rules and procedures of Articles 4, 5, 6 and 12 and the corresponding rules and procedures of the Decision, the latter shall prevail.

Article 4

Consultations

1. Members affirm their resolve to strengthen and improve the effectiveness of the consultation procedures employed by Members.

2. Each Member undertakes to accord sympathetic consideration to and afford adequate opportunity for consultation regarding any representations made by another Member concerning measures affecting the operation of any covered agreement taken within the territory of the former.[3]

3. If a request for consultations is made pursuant to a covered agreement, the Member to which the request is made shall, unless otherwise mutually agreed, reply to the request within 10 days after the date of its receipt and shall enter into consultations in good faith within a period of no more than 30 days after the date of receipt of the request, with a view to reaching a mutually satisfactory

---

[2] This paragraph shall also be applied to disputes on which panel reports have not been adopted or fully implemented.

[3] Where the provisions of any other covered agreement concerning measures taken by regional or local governments or authorities within the territory of a Member contain provisions different from the provisions of this paragraph, the provisions of such other covered agreement shall prevail.

solution. If the Member does not respond within 10 days after the date of receipt of the request, or does not enter into consultations within a period of no more than 30 days, or a period otherwise mutually agreed, after the date of receipt of the request, then the Member that requested the holding of consultations may proceed directly to request the establishment of a panel.

4. All such requests for consultations shall be notified to the DSB and the relevant Councils and Committees by the Member which requests consultations. Any request for consultations shall be submitted in writing and shall give the reasons for the request, including identification of the measures at issue and an indication of the legal basis for the complaint.

5. In the course of consultations in accordance with the provisions of a covered agreement, before resorting to further action under this Understanding, Members should attempt to obtain satisfactory adjustment of the matter.

6. Consultations shall be confidential, and without prejudice to the rights of any Member in any further proceedings.

7. If the consultations fail to settle a dispute within 60 days after the date of receipt of the request for consultations, the complaining party may request the establishment of a panel. The complaining party may request a panel during the 60-day period if the consulting parties jointly consider that consultations have failed to settle the dispute.

8. In cases of urgency, including those which concern perishable goods, Members shall enter into consultations within a period of no more than 10 days after the date of receipt of the request. If the consultations have failed to settle the dispute within a period of 20 days after the date of receipt of the request, the complaining party may request the establishment of a panel.

9. In cases of urgency, including those which concern perishable goods, the parties to the dispute, panels and the Appellate Body shall make every effort to accelerate the proceedings to the greatest extent possible.

10. During consultations Members should give special attention to the particular problems and interests of developing country Members.

11. Whenever a Member other than the consulting Members considers that it has a substantial trade interest in consultations being held pursuant to paragraph 1 of Article XXII of GATT 1994, paragraph 1 of Article XXII of GATS, or the corresponding provisions in other covered agreements,[4] such Member

---

[4] The corresponding consultation provisions in the covered agreements are listed hereunder: Agreement on Agriculture, Article 19; Agreement on the Application of Sanitary and Phytosanitary Measures, paragraph 1 of Article 11; Agreement on Textiles and Clothing, paragraph 4 of Article 8; Agreement on Technical Barriers to Trade, paragraph 1 of Article 14; Agreement on Trade-Related Investment Measures, Article 8; Agreement on Implementation of Article VI of GATT 1994, paragraph 2 of Article 17; Agreement on Implementation of Article VII of GATT 1994, paragraph 2 of Article 19; Agreement on Preshipment Inspection, Article 7; Agreement on Rules of Origin, Article 7; Agreement on Import Licensing Procedures, Article 6; Agreement on Subsidies and Countervailing Measures, Article 30; Agreement on Safeguards, Article 14; Agreement on Trade-Related Aspects of Intellectual Property Rights, Article 64.1; and any corresponding consultation provisions in Plurilateral Trade Agreements as determined by the competent bodies of each Agreement and as notified to the DSB.

may notify the consulting Members and the DSB, within 10 days after the date of the circulation of the request for consultations under said Article, of its desire to be joined in the consultations. Such Member shall be joined in the consultations, provided that the Member to which the request for consultations was addressed agrees that the claim of substantial interest is well-founded. In that event they shall so inform the DSB. If the request to be joined in the consultations is not accepted, the applicant Member shall be free to request consultations under paragraph 1 of Article XXII or paragraph 1 of Article XXIII of GATT 1994, paragraph 1 of Article XXII or paragraph 1 of Article XXIII of GATS, or the corresponding provisions in other covered agreements.

Article 5

Good offices, conciliation and mediation

1. Good offices, conciliation and mediation are procedures that are undertaken voluntarily if the parties to the dispute so agree.

2. Proceedings involving good offices, conciliation and mediation, and in particular positions taken by the parties to the dispute during these proceedings, shall be confidential, and without prejudice to the rights of either party in any further proceedings under these procedures.

3. Good offices, conciliation or mediation may be requested at any time by any party to a dispute. They may begin at any time and be terminated at any time. Once procedures for good offices, conciliation or mediation are terminated, a complaining party may then proceed with a request for the establishment of a panel.

4. When good offices, conciliation or mediation are entered into within 60 days after the date of receipt of a request for consultations, the complaining party must allow a period of 60 days after the date of receipt of the request for consultations before requesting the establishment of a panel. The complaining party may request the establishment of a panel during the 60-day period if the parties to the dispute jointly consider that the good offices, conciliation or mediation process has failed to settle the dispute.

5. If the parties to a dispute agree, procedures for good offices, conciliation or mediation may continue while the panel process proceeds.

6. The Director-General may, acting in an *ex officio* capacity, offer good offices, conciliation or mediation with the view to assisting Members to settle a dispute.

Article 6

Establishment of panels

1. If the complaining party so requests, a panel shall be established at the latest at the DSB meeting following that at which the request first appears as an

item on the DSB's agenda, unless at that meeting the DSB decides by consensus not to establish a panel.[5]

2. The request for the establishment of a panel shall be made in writing. It shall indicate whether consultations were held, identify the specific measures at issue and provide a brief summary of the legal basis of the complaint sufficient to present the problem clearly. In case the applicant requests the establishment of a panel with other than standard terms of reference, the written request shall include the proposed text of special terms of reference.

Article 7

Terms of Reference of panels

1. Panels shall have the following terms of reference unless the parties to the dispute agree otherwise within 20 days from the establishment of the panel:

> To examine, in the light of the relevant provisions in (name of the covered agreement(s) cited by the parties to the dispute), the matter referred to the DSB by (name of party) in document … and to make such findings as will assist the DSB in making the recommendations or in giving the rulings provided for in that/those agreement(s).

2. Panels shall address the relevant provisions in any covered agreement or agreements cited by the parties to the dispute.

3. In establishing a panel, the DSB may authorize its Chairman to draw up the terms of reference of the panel in consultation with the parties to the dispute, subject to the provisions of paragraph 1. The terms of reference thus drawn up shall be circulated to all Members. If other than standard terms of reference are agreed upon, any Member may raise any point relating thereto in the DSB.

Article 8

Composition of panels

1. Panels shall be composed of well-qualified governmental and/or nongovernmental individuals, including persons who have served on or presented a case to a panel, served as a representative of a Member or of a contracting party to GATT 1947 or as a representative to the Council or Committee of any covered agreement or its predecessor agreement, or in the Secretariat, taught or published on international trade law or policy, or served as a senior trade policy official of a Member.

---

[5] If the complaining party so requests, a meeting of the DSB shall be convened for this purpose within 15 days of the request, provided that at least 10 days' advance notice of the meeting is given.

2. Panel members should be selected with a view to ensuring the independence of the members, a sufficiently diverse background and a wide spectrum of experience.

3. Citizens of Members whose governments[6] are parties to the dispute or third parties as defined in paragraph 2 of Article 10 shall not serve on a panel concerned with that dispute, unless the parties to the dispute agree otherwise.

4. To assist in the selection of panelists, the Secretariat shall maintain an indicative list of governmental and non-governmental individuals possessing the qualifications outlined in paragraph 1, from which panelists may be drawn as appropriate. That list shall include the roster of non-governmental panelists established on 30 November 1984 (BISD 31S/9), and other rosters and indicative lists established under any of the covered agreements, and shall retain the names of persons on those rosters and indicative lists at the time of entry into force of the WTO Agreement. Members may periodically suggest names of governmental and non-governmental individuals for inclusion on the indicative list, providing relevant information on their knowledge of international trade and of the sectors or subject matter of the covered agreements, and those names shall be added to the list upon approval by the DSB. For each of the individuals on the list, the list shall indicate specific areas of experience or expertise of the individuals in the sectors or subject matter of the covered agreements.

5. Panels shall be composed of three panelists unless the parties to the dispute agree, within 10 days from the establishment of the panel, to a panel composed of five panelists. Members shall be informed promptly of the composition of the panel.

6. The Secretariat shall propose nominations for the panel to the parties to the dispute. The parties to the dispute shall not oppose nominations except for compelling reasons.

7. If there is no agreement on the panelists within 20 days after the date of the establishment of a panel, at the request of either party, the Director-General, in consultation with the Chairman of the DSB and the Chairman of the relevant Council or Committee, shall determine the composition of the panel by appointing the panelists whom the Director-General considers most appropriate in accordance with any relevant special or additional rules or procedures of the covered agreement or covered agreements which are at issue in the dispute, after consulting with the parties to the dispute. The Chairman of the DSB shall inform the Members of the composition of the panel thus formed no later than 10 days after the date the Chairman receives such a request.

8. Members shall undertake, as a general rule, to permit their officials to serve as panelists.

9. Panelists shall serve in their individual capacities and not as government representatives, nor as representatives of any organization. Members shall therefore

---

[6] In the case where customs unions or common markets are parties to a dispute, this provision applies to citizens of all member countries of the customs unions or common markets.

not give them instructions nor seek to influence them as individuals with regard to matters before a panel.

10. When a dispute is between a developing country Member and a developed country Member the panel shall, if the developing country Member so requests, include at least one panelist from a developing country Member.

11. Panelists' expenses, including travel and subsistence allowance, shall be met from the WTO budget in accordance with criteria to be adopted by the General Council, based on recommendations of the Committee on Budget, Finance and Administration.

Article 9

Procedures for multiple complainants

1. Where more than one Member requests the establishment of a panel related to the same matter, a single panel may be established to examine these complaints taking into account the rights of all Members concerned. A single panel should be established to examine such complaints whenever feasible.

2. The single panel shall organize its examination and present its findings to the DSB in such a manner that the rights which the parties to the dispute would have enjoyed had separate panels examined the complaints are in no way impaired. If one of the parties to the dispute so requests, the panel shall submit separate reports on the dispute concerned. The written submissions by each of the complainants shall be made available to the other complainants, and each complainant shall have the right to be present when any one of the other complainants presents its views to the panel.

3. If more than one panel is established to examine the complaints related to the same matter, to the greatest extent possible the same persons shall serve as panelists on each of the separate panels and the timetable for the panel process in such disputes shall be harmonized.

Article 10

Third parties

1. The interests of the parties to a dispute and those of other Members under a covered agreement at issue in the dispute shall be fully taken into account during the panel process.

2. Any Member having a substantial interest in a matter before a panel and having notified its interest to the DSB (referred to in this Understanding as a 'third party') shall have an opportunity to be heard by the panel and to make written submissions to the panel. These submissions shall also be given to the parties to the dispute and shall be reflected in the panel report.

3. Third parties shall receive the submissions of the parties to the dispute to the first meeting of the panel.

4. If a third party considers that a measure already the subject of a panel proceeding nullifies or impairs benefits accruing to it under any covered agreement, that Member may have recourse to normal dispute settlement procedures under this Understanding. Such a dispute shall be referred to the original panel wherever possible.

Article 11
Function of panels

The function of panels is to assist the DSB in discharging its responsibilities under this Understanding and the covered agreements. Accordingly, a panel should make an objective assessment of the matter before it, including an objective assessment of the facts of the case and the applicability of and conformity with the relevant covered agreements, and make such other findings as will assist the DSB in making the recommendations or in giving the rulings provided for in the covered agreements. Panels should consult regularly with the parties to the dispute and give them adequate opportunity to develop a mutually satisfactory solution.

Article 12
Panel procedures

1. Panels shall follow the Working Procedures in Appendix 3 unless the panel decides otherwise after consulting the parties to the dispute.

2. Panel procedures should provide sufficient flexibility so as to ensure high-quality panel reports, while not unduly delaying the panel process.

3. After consulting the parties to the dispute, the panelists shall, as soon as practicable and whenever possible within one week after the composition and terms of reference of the panel have been agreed upon, fix the timetable for the panel process, taking into account the provisions of paragraph 9 of Article 4, if relevant.

4. In determining the timetable for the panel process, the panel shall provide sufficient time for the parties to the dispute to prepare their submissions.

5. Panels should set precise deadlines for written submissions by the parties and the parties should respect those deadlines.

6. Each party to the dispute shall deposit its written submissions with the Secretariat for immediate transmission to the panel and to the other party or parties to the dispute. The complaining party shall submit its first submission in advance of the responding party's first submission unless the panel decides, in fixing the timetable referred to in paragraph 3 and after consultations with the parties to the dispute, that the parties should submit their first submissions simultaneously. When there are sequential arrangements for the deposit of first

submissions, the panel shall establish a firm time-period for receipt of the responding party's submission. Any subsequent written submissions shall be submitted simultaneously.

7. Where the parties to the dispute have failed to develop a mutually satisfactory solution, the panel shall submit its findings in the form of a written report to the DSB. In such cases, the report of a panel shall set out the findings of fact, the applicability of relevant provisions and the basic rationale behind any findings and recommendations that it makes. Where a settlement of the matter among the parties to the dispute has been found, the report of the panel shall be confined to a brief description of the case and to reporting that a solution has been reached.

8. In order to make the procedures more efficient, the period in which the panel shall conduct its examination, from the date that the composition and terms of reference of the panel have been agreed upon until the date the final report is issued to the parties to the dispute, shall, as a general rule, not exceed six months. In cases of urgency, including those relating to perishable goods, the panel shall aim to issue its report to the parties to the dispute within three months.

9. When the panel considers that it cannot issue its report within six months, or within three months in cases of urgency, it shall inform the DSB in writing of the reasons for the delay together with an estimate of the period within which it will issue its report. In no case should the period from the establishment of the panel to the circulation of the report to the Members exceed nine months.

10. In the context of consultations involving a measure taken by a developing country Member, the parties may agree to extend the periods established in paragraphs 7 and 8 of Article 4. If, after the relevant period has elapsed, the consulting parties cannot agree that the consultations have concluded, the Chairman of the DSB shall decide, after consultation with the parties, whether to extend the relevant period and, if so, for how long. In addition, in examining a complaint against a developing country Member, the panel shall accord sufficient time for the developing country Member to prepare and present its argumentation. The provisions of paragraph 1 of Article 20 and paragraph 4 of Article 21 are not affected by any action pursuant to this paragraph.

11. Where one or more of the parties is a developing country Member, the panel's report shall explicitly indicate the form in which account has been taken of relevant provisions on differential and more-favourable treatment for developing country Members that form part of the covered agreements which have been raised by the developing country Member in the course of the dispute settlement procedures.

12. The panel may suspend its work at any time at the request of the complaining party for a period not to exceed 12 months. In the event of such a suspension, the time-frames set out in paragraphs 8 and 9 of this Article, paragraph 1 of Article 20, and paragraph 4 of Article 21 shall be extended by the amount of time that the work was suspended. If the work of the panel has been

suspended for more than 12 months, the authority for establishment of the panel shall lapse.

Article 13
Right to seek information

1. Each panel shall have the right to seek information and technical advice from any individual or body which it deems appropriate. However, before a panel seeks such information or advice from any individual or body within the jurisdiction of a Member it shall inform the authorities of that Member. A Member should respond promptly and fully to any request by a panel for such information as the panel considers necessary and appropriate. Confidential information which is provided shall not be revealed without formal authorization from the individual, body, or authorities of the Member providing the information.

2. Panels may seek information from any relevant source and may consult experts to obtain their opinion on certain aspects of the matter. With respect to a factual issue concerning a scientific or other technical matter raised by a party to a dispute, a panel may request an advisory report in writing from an expert review group. Rules for the establishment of such a group and its procedures are set forth in Appendix 4.

Article 14
Confidentiality

1. Panel deliberations shall be confidential.

2. The reports of panels shall be drafted without the presence of the parties to the dispute in the light of the information provided and the statements made.

3. Opinions expressed in the panel report by individual panelists shall be anonymous.

Article 15
Interim review stage

1. Following the consideration of rebuttal submissions and oral arguments, the panel shall issue the descriptive (factual and argument) sections of its draft report to the parties to the dispute. Within a period of time set by the panel, the parties shall submit their comments in writing.

2. Following the expiration of the set period of time for receipt of comments from the parties to the dispute, the panel shall issue an interim report to the parties, including both the descriptive sections and the panel's findings and conclusions. Within a period of time set by the panel, a party may submit a written request for the panel to review precise aspects of the interim report prior to

circulation of the final report to the Members. At the request of a party, the panel shall hold a further meeting with the parties on the issues identified in the written comments. If no comments are received from any party within the comment period, the interim report shall be considered the final panel report and circulated promptly to the Members.

3. The findings of the final panel report shall include a discussion of the arguments made at the interim review stage. The interim review stage shall be conducted within the time-period set out in paragraph 8 of Article 12.

Article 16

Adoption of panel reports

1. In order to provide sufficient time for the Members to consider panel reports, the reports shall not be considered for adoption by the DSB until 20 days after the date they have been circulated to the Members.

2. Members having objections to a panel report shall give written reasons to explain their objections for circulation at least 10 days prior to the DSB meeting at which the panel report will be considered.

3. The parties to a dispute shall have the right to participate fully in the consideration of the panel report by the DSB, and their views shall be fully recorded.

4. Within 60 days after the date of circulation of a panel report to the Members, the report shall be adopted at a DSB meeting[7] unless a party to the dispute formally notifies the DSB of its decision to appeal or the DSB decides by consensus not to adopt the report. If a party has notified its decision to appeal, the report by the panel shall not be considered for adoption by the DSB until after completion of the appeal. This adoption procedure is without prejudice to the right of Members to express their views on a panel report.

Article 17

Appellate review

Standing Appellate Body

1. A standing Appellate Body shall be established by the DSB. The Appellate Body shall hear appeals from panel cases. It shall be composed of seven persons, three of whom shall serve on any one case. Persons serving on the Appellate Body shall serve in rotation. Such rotation shall be determined in the working procedures of the Appellate Body.

2. The DSB shall appoint persons to serve on the Appellate Body for a four-year term, and each person may be reappointed once. However, the terms of

---

[7] If a meeting of the DSB is not scheduled within this period at a time that enables the requirements of paragraphs 1 and 4 of Article 16 to be met, a meeting of the DSB shall be held for this purpose.

three of the seven persons appointed immediately after the entry into force of the WTO Agreement shall expire at the end of two years, to be determined by lot. Vacancies shall be filled as they arise. A person appointed to replace a person whose term of office has not expired shall hold office for the remainder of the predecessor's term.

3. The Appellate Body shall comprise persons of recognized authority, with demonstrated expertise in law, international trade and the subject matter of the covered agreements generally. They shall be unaffiliated with any government. The Appellate Body membership shall be broadly representative of membership in the WTO. All persons serving on the Appellate Body shall be available at all times and on short notice, and shall stay abreast of dispute settlement activities and other relevant activities of the WTO. They shall not participate in the consideration of any disputes that would create a direct or indirect conflict of interest.

4. Only parties to the dispute, not third parties, may appeal a panel report. Third parties which have notified the DSB of a substantial interest in the matter pursuant to paragraph 2 of Article 10 may make written submissions to, and be given an opportunity to be heard by, the Appellate Body.

5. As a general rule, the proceedings shall not exceed 60 days from the date a party to the dispute formally notifies its decision to appeal to the date the Appellate Body circulates its report. In fixing its timetable the Appellate Body shall take into account the provisions of paragraph 9 of Article 4, if relevant. When the Appellate Body considers that it cannot provide its report within 60 days, it shall inform the DSB in writing of the reasons for the delay together with an estimate of the period within which it will submit its report. In no case shall the proceedings exceed 90 days.

6. An appeal shall be limited to issues of law covered in the panel report and legal interpretations developed by the panel.

7. The Appellate Body shall be provided with appropriate administrative and legal support as it requires.

8. The expenses of persons serving on the Appellate Body, including travel and subsistence allowance, shall be met from the WTO budget in accordance with criteria to be adopted by the General Council, based on recommendations of the Committee on Budget, Finance and Administration.

Procedures for appellate review

9. Working procedures shall be drawn up by the Appellate Body in consultation with the Chairman of the DSB and the Director-General, and communicated to the Members for their information.

10. The proceedings of the Appellate Body shall be confidential. The reports of the Appellate Body shall be drafted without the presence of the parties to the dispute and in the light of the information provided and the statements made.

11. Opinions expressed in the Appellate Body report by individuals serving on the Appellate Body shall be anonymous.

12. The Appellate Body shall address each of the issues raised in accordance with paragraph 6 during the appellate proceeding.

13. The Appellate Body may uphold, modify or reverse the legal findings and conclusions of the panel.

Adoption of Appellate Body reports

14. An Appellate Body report shall be adopted by the DSB and unconditionally accepted by the parties to the dispute unless the DSB decides by consensus not to adopt the Appellate Body report within 30 days following its circulation to the Members.[8] This adoption procedure is without prejudice to the right of Members to express their views on an Appellate Body report.

Article 18

Communications with the panel or Appellate Body

1. There shall be no *ex parte* communications with the panel or Appellate Body concerning matters under consideration by the panel or Appellate Body.

2. Written submissions to the panel or the Appellate Body shall be treated as confidential, but shall be made available to the parties to the dispute. Nothing in this Understanding shall preclude a party to a dispute from disclosing statements of its own positions to the public. Members shall treat as confidential information submitted by another Member to the panel or the Appellate Body which that Member has designated as confidential. A party to a dispute shall also, upon request of a Member, provide a non-confidential summary of the information contained in its written submissions that could be disclosed to the public.

Article 19

Panel and Appellate Body recommendations

1. Where a panel or the Appellate Body concludes that a measure is inconsistent with a covered agreement, it shall recommend that the Member concerned[9] bring the measure into conformity with that agreement.[10] In addition to its recommendations, the panel or Appellate Body may suggest ways in which the Member concerned could implement the recommendations.

---

[8] If a meeting of the DSB is not scheduled during this period, such a meeting of the DSB shall be held for this purpose.

[9] The 'Member concerned' is the party to the dispute to which the panel or Appellate Body recommendations are directed.

[10] With respect to recommendations in cases not involving a violation of GATT 1994 or any other covered agreement, see Article 26.

2. In accordance with paragraph 2 of Article 3, in their findings and recommendations, the panel and Appellate Body cannot add to or diminish the rights and obligations provided in the covered agreements.

Article 20
Time-frame for DSB decisions

Unless otherwise agreed to by the parties to the dispute, the period from the date of establishment of the panel by the DSB until the date the DSB considers the panel or appellate report for adoption shall as a general rule not exceed nine months where the panel report is not appealed or 12 months where the report is appealed. Where either the panel or the Appellate Body has acted, pursuant to paragraph 9 of Article 12 or paragraph 5 of Article 17, to extend the time for providing its report, the additional time taken shall be added to the above periods.

Article 21
Surveillance of implementation of recommendations and rulings

1. Prompt compliance with recommendations or rulings of the DSB is essential in order to ensure effective resolution of disputes to the benefit of all Members.

2. Particular attention should be paid to matters affecting the interests of developing country Members with respect to measures which have been subject to dispute settlement.

3. At a DSB meeting held within 30 days[11] after the date of adoption of the panel or Appellate Body report, the Member concerned shall inform the DSB of its intentions in respect of implementation of the recommendations and rulings of the DSB. If it is impracticable to comply immediately with the recommendations and rulings, the Member concerned shall have a reasonable period of time in which to do so. The reasonable period of time shall be:

(a) the period of time proposed by the Member concerned, provided that such period is approved by the DSB; or, in the absence of such approval,
(b) a period of time mutually agreed by the parties to the dispute within 45 days after the date of adoption of the recommendations and rulings; or, in the absence of such agreement,
(c) a period of time determined through binding arbitration within 90 days after the date of adoption of the recommendations and rulings.[12] In such

---

[11] If a meeting of the DSB is not scheduled during this period, such a meeting of the DSB shall be held for this purpose.

[12] If the parties cannot agree on an arbitrator within ten days after referring the matter to arbitration, the arbitrator shall be appointed by the Director-General within ten days, after consulting the parties.

arbitration, a guideline for the arbitrator[13] should be that the reasonable period of time to implement panel or Appellate Body recommendations should not exceed 15 months from the date of adoption of a panel or Appellate Body report. However, that time may be shorter or longer, depending upon the particular circumstances.

4. Except where the panel or the Appellate Body has extended, pursuant to paragraph 9 of Article 12 or paragraph 5 of Article 17, the time of providing its report, the period from the date of establishment of the panel by the DSB until the date of determination of the reasonable period of time shall not exceed 15 months unless the parties to the dispute agree otherwise. Where either the panel or the Appellate Body has acted to extend the time of providing its report, the additional time taken shall be added to the 15-month period; provided that unless the parties to the dispute agree that there are exceptional circumstances, the total time shall not exceed 18 months.

5. Where there is disagreement as to the existence or consistency with a covered agreement of measures taken to comply with the recommendations and rulings such dispute shall be decided through recourse to these dispute settlement procedures, including wherever possible resort to the original panel. The panel shall circulate its report within 90 days after the date of referral of the matter to it. When the panel considers that it cannot provide its report within this time frame, it shall inform the DSB in writing of the reasons for the delay together with an estimate of the period within which it will submit its report.

6. The DSB shall keep under surveillance the implementation of adopted recommendations or rulings. The issue of implementation of the recommendations or rulings may be raised at the DSB by any Member at any time following their adoption. Unless the DSB decides otherwise, the issue of implementation of the recommendations or rulings shall be placed on the agenda of the DSB meeting after six months following the date of establishment of the reasonable period of time pursuant to paragraph 3 and shall remain on the DSB's agenda until the issue is resolved. At least 10 days prior to each such DSB meeting, the Member concerned shall provide the DSB with a status report in writing of its progress in the implementation of the recommendations or rulings.

7. If the matter is one which has been raised by a developing country Member, the DSB shall consider what further action it might take which would be appropriate to the circumstances.

8. If the case is one brought by a developing country Member, in considering what appropriate action might be taken, the DSB shall take into account not only the trade coverage of measures complained of, but also their impact on the economy of developing country Members concerned.

---

[13] The expression 'arbitrator' shall be interpreted as referring either to an individual or a group.

Article 22

Compensation and the suspension of concessions

1. Compensation and the suspension of concessions or other obligations are temporary measures available in the event that the recommendations and rulings are not implemented within a reasonable period of time. However, neither compensation nor the suspension of concessions or other obligations is preferred to full implementation of a recommendation to bring a measure into conformity with the covered agreements. Compensation is voluntary and, if granted, shall be consistent with the covered agreements.

2. If the Member concerned fails to bring the measure found to be inconsistent with a covered agreement into compliance therewith or otherwise comply with the recommendations and rulings within the reasonable period of time determined pursuant to paragraph 3 of Article 21, such Member shall, if so requested, and no later than the expiry of the reasonable period of time, enter into negotiations with any party having invoked the dispute settlement procedures, with a view to developing mutually acceptable compensation. If no satisfactory compensation has been agreed within 20 days after the date of expiry of the reasonable period of time, any party having invoked the dispute settlement procedures may request authorization from the DSB to suspend the application to the Member concerned of concessions or other obligations under the covered agreements.

3. In considering what concessions or other obligations to suspend, the complaining party shall apply the following principles and procedures:

(a) the general principle is that the complaining party should first seek to suspend concessions or other obligations with respect to the same sector(s) as that in which the panel or Appellate Body has found a violation or other nullification or impairment;

(b) if that party considers that it is not practicable or effective to suspend concessions or other obligations with respect to the same sector(s), it may seek to suspend concessions or other obligations in other sectors under the same agreement;

(c) if that party considers that it is not practicable or effective to suspend concessions or other obligations with respect to other sectors under the same agreement, and that the circumstances are serious enough, it may seek to suspend concessions or other obligations under another covered agreement;

(d) in applying the above principles, that party shall take into account:

   (i) the trade in the sector or under the agreement under which the panel or Appellate Body has found a violation or other nullification or impairment, and the importance of such trade to that party;

   (ii) the broader economic elements related to the nullification or impairment and the broader economic consequences of the suspension of concessions or other obligations;

(e) if that party decides to request authorization to suspend concessions or other obligations pursuant to subparagraphs (b) or (c), it shall state the reasons therefor in its request. At the same time as the request is forwarded to the DSB, it also shall be forwarded to the relevant Councils and also, in the case of a request pursuant to subparagraph (b), the relevant sectoral bodies;

(f) for purposes of this paragraph, 'sector' means:
   (i) with respect to goods, all goods;
   (ii) with respect to services, a principal sector as identified in the current 'Services Sectoral Classification List' which identifies such sectors;[14]
   (iii) with respect to trade-related intellectual property rights, each of the categories of intellectual property rights covered in Section 1, or Section 2, or Section 3, or Section 4, or Section 5, or Section 6, or Section 7 of Part II, or the obligations under Part III, or Part IV of the Agreement on TRIPS;

(g) for purposes of this paragraph, 'agreement' means:
   (i) with respect to goods, the agreements listed in Annex 1A of the WTO Agreement, taken as a whole as well as the Plurilateral Trade Agreements in so far as the relevant parties to the dispute are parties to these agreements;
   (ii) with respect to services, the GATS;
   (iii) with respect to intellectual property rights, the Agreement on TRIPS.

4. The level of the suspension of concessions or other obligations authorized by the DSB shall be equivalent to the level of the nullification or impairment.

5. The DSB shall not authorize suspension of concessions or other obligations if a covered agreement prohibits such suspension.

6. When the situation described in paragraph 2 occurs, the DSB, upon request, shall grant authorization to suspend concessions or other obligations within 30 days of the expiry of the reasonable period of time unless the DSB decides by consensus to reject the request. However, if the Member concerned objects to the level of suspension proposed, or claims that the principles and procedures set forth in paragraph 3 have not been followed where a complaining party has requested authorization to suspend concessions or other obligations pursuant to paragraph 3(b) or (c), the matter shall be referred to arbitration. Such arbitration shall be carried out by the original panel, if members are available, or by an arbitrator[15] appointed by the Director-General and shall be completed within 60 days after the date of expiry of the reasonable period of time. Concessions or other obligations shall not be suspended during the course of the arbitration.

7. The arbitrator[16] acting pursuant to paragraph 6 shall not examine the nature of the concessions or other obligations to be suspended but shall determine

---

[14] The list in document MTN.GNS/W/120 identifies eleven sectors.
[15] The expression 'arbitrator' shall be interpreted as referring either to an individual or a group.
[16] The expression 'arbitrator' shall be interpreted as referring either to an individual or a group or to the members of the original panel when serving in the capacity of arbitrator.

whether the level of such suspension is equivalent to the level of nullification or impairment. The arbitrator may also determine if the proposed suspension of concessions or other obligations is allowed under the covered agreement. However, if the matter referred to arbitration includes a claim that the principles and procedures set forth in paragraph 3 have not been followed, the arbitrator shall examine that claim. In the event the arbitrator determines that those principles and procedures have not been followed, the complaining party shall apply them consistent with paragraph 3. The parties shall accept the arbitrator's decision as final and the parties concerned shall not seek a second arbitration. The DSB shall be informed promptly of the decision of the arbitrator and shall upon request, grant authorization to suspend concessions or other obligations where the request is consistent with the decision of the arbitrator, unless the DSB decides by consensus to reject the request.

8. The suspension of concessions or other obligations shall be temporary and shall only be applied until such time as the measure found to be inconsistent with a covered agreement has been removed, or the Member that must implement recommendations or rulings provides a solution to the nullification or impairment of benefits, or a mutually satisfactory solution is reached. In accordance with paragraph 6 of Article 21, the DSB shall continue to keep under surveillance the implementation of adopted recommendations or rulings, including those cases where compensation has been provided or concessions or other obligations have been suspended but the recommendations to bring a measure into conformity with the covered agreements have not been implemented.

9. The dispute settlement provisions of the covered agreements may be invoked in respect of measures affecting their observance taken by regional or local governments or authorities within the territory of a Member. When the DSB has ruled that a provision of a covered agreement has not been observed, the responsible Member shall take such reasonable measures as may be available to it to ensure its observance. The provisions of the covered agreements and this Understanding relating to compensation and suspension of concessions or other obligations apply in cases where it has not been possible to secure such observance.[17]

Article 23

Strengthening of the multilateral system

1. When Members seek the redress of a violation of obligations or other nullification or impairment of benefits under the covered agreements or an impediment to the attainment of any objective of the covered agreements, they shall have recourse to, and abide by, the rules and procedures of this Understanding.

---

[17] Where the provisions of any covered agreement concerning measures taken by regional or local governments or authorities within the territory of a Member contain provisions different from the provisions of this paragraph, the provisions of such covered agreement shall prevail.

2. In such cases, Members shall:

(a) not make a determination to the effect that a violation has occurred, that benefits have been nullified or impaired or that the attainment of any objective of the covered agreements has been impeded, except through recourse to dispute settlement in accordance with the rules and procedures of this Understanding, and shall make any such determination consistent with the findings contained in the panel or Appellate Body report adopted by the DSB or an arbitration award rendered under this Understanding;

(b) follow the procedures set forth in Article 21 to determine the reasonable period of time for the Member concerned to implement the recommendations and rulings; and

(c) follow the procedures set forth in Article 22 to determine the level of suspension of concessions or other obligations and obtain DSB authorization in accordance with those procedures before suspending concessions or other obligations under the covered agreements in response to the failure of the Member concerned to implement the recommendations and rulings within that reasonable period of time.

Article 24

Special Procedures involving least-developed country members

1. At all stages of the determination of the causes of a dispute and of dispute settlement procedures involving a least-developed country Member, particular consideration shall be given to the special situation of least-developed country Members. In this regard, Members shall exercise due restraint in raising matters under these procedures involving a least-developed country Member. If nullification or impairment is found to result from a measure taken by a least-developed country Member, complaining parties shall exercise due restraint in asking for compensation or seeking authorization to suspend the application of concessions or other obligations pursuant to these procedures.

2. In dispute settlement cases involving a least-developed country Member, where a satisfactory solution has not been found in the course of consultations the Director-General or the Chairman of the DSB shall, upon request by a least-developed country Member offer their good offices, conciliation and mediation with a view to assisting the parties to settle the dispute, before a request for a panel is made. The Director-General or the Chairman of the DSB, in providing the above assistance, may consult any source which either deems appropriate.

Article 25

Arbitration

1. Expeditious arbitration within the WTO as an alternative means of dispute settlement can facilitate the solution of certain disputes that concern issues that are clearly defined by both parties.

2. Except as otherwise provided in this Understanding, resort to arbitration shall be subject to mutual agreement of the parties which shall agree on the procedures to be followed. Agreements to resort to arbitration shall be notified to all Members sufficiently in advance of the actual commencement of the arbitration process.

3. Other Members may become party to an arbitration proceeding only upon the agreement of the parties which have agreed to have recourse to arbitration. The parties to the proceeding shall agree to abide by the arbitration award. Arbitration awards shall be notified to the DSB and the Council or Committee of any relevant agreement where any Member may raise any point relating thereto.

4. Articles 21 and 22 of this Understanding shall apply *mutatis mutandis* to arbitration awards.

Article 26

1.*Non-Violation Complaints of the Type Described in Paragraph 1(b) of Article XXIII of GATT 1994*: Where the provisions of paragraph 1(b) of Article XXIII of GATT 1994 are applicable to a covered agreement, a panel or the Appellate Body may only make rulings and recommendations where a party to the dispute considers that any benefit accruing to it directly or indirectly under the relevant covered agreement is being nullified or impaired or the attainment of any objective of that Agreement is being impeded as a result of the application by a Member of any measure, whether or not it conflicts with the provisions of that Agreement. Where and to the extent that such party considers and a panel or the Appellate Body determines that a case concerns a measure that does not conflict with the provisions of a covered agreement to which the provisions of paragraph 1(b) of Article XXIII of GATT 1994 are applicable, the procedures in this Understanding shall apply, subject to the following:

(a) the complaining party shall present a detailed justification in support of any complaint relating to a measure which does not conflict with the relevant covered agreement;

(b) where a measure has been found to nullify or impair benefits under, or impede the attainment of objectives, of the relevant covered agreement without violation thereof, there is no obligation to withdraw the measure. However, in such cases, the panel or the Appellate Body shall recommend that the Member concerned make a mutually satisfactory adjustment;

(c) notwithstanding the provisions of Article 21, the arbitration provided for in paragraph 3 of Article 21, upon request of either party, may include a determination of the level of benefits which have been nullified or impaired, and may also suggest ways and means of reaching a mutually satisfactory adjustment; such suggestions shall not be binding upon the parties to the dispute;

(d) notwithstanding the provisions of paragraph 1 of Article 22, compensation may be part of a mutually satisfactory adjustment as final settlement of the dispute.

2. *Complaints of the Type Described in Paragraph 1(c) of Article XXIII of GATT 1994*: Where the provisions of paragraph 1(c) of Article XXIII of GATT 1994 are applicable to a covered agreement, a panel may only make rulings and recommendations where a party considers that any benefit accruing to it directly or indirectly under the relevant covered agreement is being nullified or impaired or the attainment of any objective of that Agreement is being impeded as a result of the existence of any situation other than those to which the provisions of paragraphs 1(a) and 1(b) of Article XXIII of GATT 1994 are applicable. Where and to the extent that such party considers and a panel determines that the matter is covered by this paragraph, the procedures of this Understanding shall apply only up to and including the point in the proceedings where the panel report has been circulated to the Members. The dispute settlement rules and procedures contained in the Decision of 12 April 1989 (BISD 36S/61–67) shall apply to consideration for adoption, and surveillance and implementation of recommendations and rulings. The following shall also apply:

(a) the complaining party shall present a detailed justification in support of any argument made with respect to issues covered under this paragraph;
(b) in cases involving matters covered by this paragraph, if a panel finds that cases also involve dispute settlement matters other than those covered by this paragraph, the panel shall circulate a report to the DSB addressing any such matters and a separate report on matters falling under this paragraph.

Article 27

Responsibilities of the Secretariat

1. The Secretariat shall have the responsibility of assisting panels, especially on the legal, historical and procedural aspects of the matters dealt with, and of providing secretarial and technical support.

2. While the Secretariat assists Members in respect of dispute settlement at their request, there may also be a need to provide additional legal advice and assistance in respect of dispute settlement to developing country Members. To this end, the Secretariat shall make available a qualified legal expert from the WTO technical cooperation services to any developing country Member which so requests. This expert shall assist the developing country Member in a manner ensuring the continued impartiality of the Secretariat.

3. The Secretariat shall conduct special training courses for interested Members concerning these dispute settlement procedures and practices so as to enable Members' experts to be better informed in this regard.

Appendices

Appendix 1: Agreements Covered by the Understanding

(A) Agreement Establishing the World Trade Organization
(B) Multilateral Trade Agreements

> Annex 1A: Multilateral Agreements on Trade in Goods
> Annex 1B: General Agreement on Trade in Services
> Annex 1C: Agreement on Trade-Related Aspects of Intellectual Property Rights
> Annex 2:   Understanding on Rules and Procedures Governing the Settlement of Disputes

(C) Plurilateral Trade Agreements

> Annex 4:   Agreement on Trade in Civil Aircraft
> Agreement on Government Procurement
> International Dairy Agreement
> International Bovine Meat Agreement

The applicability of this Understanding to the Plurilateral Trade Agreements shall be subject to the adoption of a decision by the parties to each agreement setting out the terms for the application of the Understanding to the individual agreement, including any special or additional rules or procedures for inclusion in Appendix 2, as notified to the DSB.

Appendix 2: Special or Additional Rules and Procedures Contained in the Covered Agreements

Agreement	Rules and Procedures
Agreement on the Application of Sanitary and Phytosanitary Measures	11.2
Agreement on Textiles and Clothing	2.14, 2.21, 4.4, 5.2, 5.4, 5.6, 6.9, 6.10, 6.11, 8.1 through 8.12
Agreement on Technical Barriers to Trade	14.2 through 14.4, Annex 2
Agreement on Implementation of Article VI of GATT 1994	17.4 through 17.7

Agreement on Implementation of Article VII of GATT 1994	19.3 through 19.5, Annex II.2(f), 3, 9, 21
Agreement on Subsidies and Countervailing Measures	4.2 through 4.12, 6.6, 7.2 through 7.10, 8.5, footnote 35, 24.4, 27.7, Annex V
General Agreement on Trade in Services	XXII:3, XXIII:3
Annex on Financial Services	4
Annex on Air Transport Services	4
Decision on Certain Dispute Settlement Procedures for the GATS	1 through 5

The list of rules and procedures in this Appendix includes provisions where only a part of the provision may be relevant in this context.

Any special or additional rules or procedures in the Plurilateral Trade Agreements as determined by the competent bodies of each agreement and as notified to the DSB.

Appendix 3: Working Procedures

1. In its proceedings the panel shall follow the relevant provisions of this Understanding. In addition, the following working procedures shall apply.

2. The panel shall meet in closed session. The parties to the dispute, and interested parties, shall be present at the meetings only when invited by the panel to appear before it.

3. The deliberations of the panel and the documents submitted to it shall be kept confidential. Nothing in this Understanding shall preclude a party to a dispute from disclosing statements of its own positions to the public. Members shall treat as confidential information submitted by another Member to the panel which that Member has designated as confidential. Where a party to a dispute submits a confidential version of its written submissions to the panel, it shall also, upon request of a Member, provide a non-confidential summary of the information contained in its submissions that could be disclosed to the public.

4. Before the first substantive meeting of the panel with the parties, the parties to the dispute shall transmit to the panel written submissions in which they present the facts of the case and their arguments.

5. At its first substantive meeting with the parties, the panel shall ask the party which has brought the complaint to present its case. Subsequently, and still at the same meeting, the party against which the complaint has been brought shall be asked to present its point of view.

6. All third parties which have notified their interest in the dispute to the DSB shall be invited in writing to present their views during a session of the first substantive meeting of the panel set aside for that purpose. All such third parties may be present during the entirety of this session.

7. Formal rebuttals shall be made at a second substantive meeting of the panel. The party complained against shall have the right to take the floor first to be followed by the complaining party. The parties shall submit, prior to that meeting, written rebuttals to the panel.

8. The panel may at any time put questions to the parties and ask them for explanations either in the course of a meeting with the parties or in writing.

9. The parties to the dispute and any third party invited to present its views in accordance with Article 10 shall make available to the panel a written version of their oral statements.

10. In the interest of full transparency, the presentations, rebuttals and statements referred to in paragraphs 5 to 9 shall be made in the presence of the parties. Moreover, each party's written submissions, including any comments on the descriptive part of the report and responses to questions put by the panel, shall be made available to the other party or parties.

11. Any additional procedures specific to the panel.

12. Proposed timetable for panel work:

(a) Receipt of first written submissions of the parties:
  (1) complaining party: 3–6 weeks
  (2) Party complained against: 2–3 weeks
(b) Date, time and place of first substantive meeting with the
    parties; third party session: 1–2 weeks
(c) Receipt of written rebuttals of the parties: 2–3 weeks
(d) Date, time and place of second substantive meeting with the
    parties: 1–2 weeks
(e) Issuance of descriptive part of the report to the parties: 2–4 weeks
(f) Receipt of comments by the parties on the descriptive
    part of the report: 2 weeks
(g) Issuance of the interim report, including the findings and
    conclusions, to the parties: 2–4 weeks
(h) Deadline for party to request review of part(s) of report: 1 week
(i) Period of review by panel, including possible additional
    meeting with parties: 2 weeks
(j) Issuance of final report to parties to dispute: 2 weeks
(k) Circulation of the final report to the Members: 3 weeks

The above calendar may be changed in the light of unforeseen developments. Additional meetings with the parties shall be scheduled if required.

Appendix 4: Expert Review Groups

The following rules and procedures shall apply to expert review groups established in accordance with the provisions of paragraph 2 of Article 13.

1. Expert review groups are under the panel's authority. Their terms of reference and detailed working procedures shall be decided by the panel, and they shall report to the panel.

2. Participation in expert review groups shall be restricted to persons of professional standing and experience in the field in question.

3. Citizens of parties to the dispute shall not serve on an expert review group without the joint agreement of the parties to the dispute, except in exceptional circumstances when the panel considers that the need for specialized scientific expertise cannot be fulfilled otherwise. Government officials of parties to the dispute shall not serve on an expert review group. Members of expert review groups shall serve in their individual capacities and not as government representatives, nor as representatives of any organization. Governments or organizations shall therefore not give them instructions with regard to matters before an expert review group.

4. Expert review groups may consult and seek information and technical advice from any source they deem appropriate. Before an expert review group seeks such information or advice from a source within the jurisdiction of a Member, it shall inform the government of that Member. Any Member shall respond promptly and fully to any request by an expert review group for such information as the expert review group considers necessary and appropriate.

5. The parties to a dispute shall have access to all relevant information provided to an expert review group, unless it is of a confidential nature. Confidential information provided to the expert review group shall not be released without formal authorization from the government, organization or person providing the information. Where such information is requested from the expert review group but release of such information by the expert review group is not authorized, a non-confidential summary of the information will be provided by the government, organization or person supplying the information.

6. The expert review group shall submit a draft report to the parties to the dispute with a view to obtaining their comments, and taking them into account, as appropriate, in the final report, which shall also be issued to the parties to the dispute when it is submitted to the panel. The final report of the expert review group shall be advisory only.

Index